Acting Up

Dave Hopwood

National Society/Church House Publishing

National Society/Church House Publishing
Church House,
Great Smith Street,
London SW1P 3NZ

ISBN 0 7151 4866 4

First published in 1995 by The National Society and Church House Publishing

Reprinted 1997

Performing Rights

Photocopying

Text design and typesetting by Church House Publishing
Cover design by Leigh Hurlock
Print arranged by Indeprint Print Production Services
Printed by Bell and Bain Ltd, Glasgow

Contents

Introduction

Drama – why bother? When we consider drama and the Bible we tend to think of the parables. Jesus told stories – dramatic, surprising, disturbing stories. It was his main form of teaching. (It seems he wasn't too hot on three-point sermons.) However, the more I have read the Bible the more I have discovered that the whole book is packed with drama. The psalms literally drip with dramatic pictures and images: 'my life is disappearing like smoke' (Psalm 102 verse 3); 'we grow and flourish like a wild flower' (Psalm 103 verse 15); 'we have escaped like a bird from a hunter's trap' (Psalm 124 verse 7); 'my whole being desires you, like a dry, worn-out, and waterless land' (Psalm 63 verse 1); 'my pillow is soaked with tears' (Psalm 6 verse 6); 'my strength . . . drained, as moisture is dried up by the summer heat' (Psalm 32 verse 4).

Time and time again we are presented with rich, visual imagery and parables. *Proverbs* is the same, the messages of the prophets too. Imagine Noah for a moment, perhaps the longest piece of street theatre ever – the building of a massive boat to demonstrate to people that soon they were in danger of drowning. Talking of street theatre take a look at Ezekiel – God tells this man stories which he then takes on the street. Why does God use drama? Because it seems to make perfect sense. God understands what will communicate, he knows the things which will strike home – and when we look at the Bible and the teaching of Jesus there is always drama at the heart of it.

Stories and imagery encourage us to remember and enable us to learn. But all that takes practise! The need today for an audio-visual message is greater than ever. Cinema attendance is booming, interactive TV is the talk of the moment. Adverts are more like mini soap operas, and you can't just record a song these days, you have to have the video to sell it. We are surrounded by the visual image. Let's get in on the act!

When Jesus wanted to make the point about being childlike he didn't merely talk about it – he used a living, breathing, kicking illustration. But this kind of communication does require careful preparation and thought. The message will best communicate when it is draped in style. I am sure that Jesus' stories were quite different to anything folks had ever heard before, and Jesus told them well. You never find him starting a story like this: 'Now there was a man who had two sons – or was it three . . . ' No. Jesus was prepared, he delivered his material effectively and in an arresting style. This takes thought and preparation, but it is important, and it is worth it. This book contains some quite visual sketches, not only dialogues, but physical drama. The saying goes: 'a picture communicates a thousand words'; some of these pieces are full of physical pictures.

There are four response stories – an easy way to involve your whole church in a sketch. There are group mimes for those not so keen on learning lines – and if you're a drama group of one there are a couple of monologues lurking between the sketches and response stories. I thoroughly recommend the use of drama to you – it's the stuff of the gospel, and it can enrich church life and communication. Go for it.

In the Beginning

Part I is based on part of Genesis chapter 1 and looks at the creation of the world. It may be used as a piece on its own.

Part II looks at the fall and the coming of Jesus.

Cast   Narrator
A group of four to twelve people who illustrate the narration with mime pictures and the occasional sound effect

Part I

Begin with the group in a line facing the audience.

Narrator   In the beginning there was chaos

(Out of time rhythm, clapping or beating hands on chest or legs)

And God brought order.

(Strict rhythm)

He created the heavens

(Look up)

And the earth;

(Look down)

And it was good.

(Smile, shake hands)

The earth produced all kinds of plants and vegetation.

(Half the group become different kinds of trees)

Bearing grain and fruit

(The other half pluck fruit and eat it noisily)

And God saw that this was good.

(Smile, shake hands with enthusiasm)

He created the sun,

(Shout 'Read all about it!')

The moon

(Howl like wolves)

And the stars,

('Film stars' step forward and throw kisses, others applaud)

To light up the night

(Fall asleep)

And the day;

(Wake up, bright and cheerful)

And he was pleased with what he had made.

(Shake hands, slap backs)

Then he formed many creatures to fill the earth.
All kinds of animals,

(Farmyard animal noises)

Fish,

(Open and close mouth – goldfish style)

And birds.

(Girls pose like models on a catwalk – men wolf whistle)

He blessed them and commanded them to multiply

(Count on calculators and fingers)

For what he had created was good.

(Pat backs, shake hands, etc.)

Then God created man –

(Men step forward and pose)

And woman.

(Women shove them aside and pose)

He gave them control of the earth –

(All hold out hands in sweeping motion)

Over the trees and the plants;

(Tree poses)

Over the animals,

(Farmyard sounds)

and fish,

(Fish mouths)

and birds.

(Girls posing)

> God looked at everything that he had made and he was pleased,

(Slap backs, hands, jump, laugh)

> For the world was good.
> And then he rested, for his creation was complete.

(All rest, lean on each other)

Part II

Narrator   And while God rested, man began destroying his world –

(Aggressive expressions)

> The sun, the stars,
> The animals and trees;

(Group adopt destructive poses)

> And what God had created as good

(All smile, look happy, laugh)

> Man used for evil.

(All snarl angrily)

> God wept over his world

(Bury head in hands)

> Which was heading for chaos,

(Create an out of time rhythm, clapping or hitting hand on chest or legs)

> Because man's heart had been corrupted.

(Rhythm becomes a steady heartbeat, hands slapping chest)

> So God decided

(Heartbeat continues during this sequence)

> That he himself should visit this world –
> To live as a man,

(Appropriate poses should be adopted, two of the group maintain the heartbeat)

To laugh and cry as a man.

(Laughter)

To eat, drink, and talk as a man.

(Eating and conversation)

And in the end – to die

(Heartbeat stops; all look stage front, shocked)

As a man.

(All freeze)

Jacob's Ladder

The account from Genesis chapters 27 and 28 where Jacob tricks his father into giving him the blessing due to his elder brother, then later has a vision of angels going up to heaven and hears God's voice. This also explores the theme of giving to God.

It is suitable for performance by children to an adult audience although it could also be performed to children.

Cast   Narrator

A group of three to six people who follow the stage directions in brackets and from whom the following speakers come:

    Grabber 1
    Grabber 2
    Eater
    Cook
    God (tallest member of the group)

Begin with the narrator standing or sitting stage right. The group sit on the floor, frozen as if in discussion.

Narrator   There was once a man called Jacob.

(Group stand, wave and smile at audience)

His name meant – 'One who grabs'.

(Smiles change to snarls, group grab and say 'Gimme that!')

And all through his life he cheated other people.

Grabber 1   You've eaten my sweets!

Grabber 2   Well, you pinched my socks.

Grabber 1   No one would want your socks!

(This then degenerates into a full blown argument. Freeze)

He even cheated his own brother Esau out of his birthright – for a mere bowl of stew.

Eater   I'm starving. I'd give my birthright for a bowl of hedgehog stew!

Cook   *(Turns round with a saucepan in hand)*
I thought you'd never offer!

(Mimes pouring a ladle of stew into the Eater's hands. The others watch in horror. They all freeze.)

> Now one day, Jacob was running away to his uncle's in order to escape from Esau . . .

(Group turn and step)

> Who wanted to kill him.

(Group draw finger across throat, with appropriate sound effect)

> Jacob was in a bad way!

('Oh, oh!' Thumbs down)

> He didn't have much time for God – because he didn't think God had much time for him. After all – he was just a grabber.

(Snarl and grab, 'Gimme that!')

> Soon, he came to a place called Bethel,

(Two of group form a sign post, arms out. Third person scratches their head and reads it. The others look on and shrug)

> Where he decided to rest.

(Yawn, lean on sign post)

> So he lay down, and fell asleep.

(Group all sleep with their heads resting on their arms)

> And while he slept, he had a dream . . . a very unusual dream.

(One of group becomes an angel, smiling, and pointing to their halo, saying 'Ding!')

> He saw an angel . . . in fact, lots of angels.

(All become angels)

> And they were climbing a ladder to heaven.

(Angels freeze, stepping onto ladders)

> And the Lord was there too, standing right beside Jacob.

(God stands, possibly on a chair, looking down on the others – who look up in amazement.)

God   Jacob, listen to me. I care about you. I love you.

Narrator   Said the Lord.

God   I will always be with you and protect you – all my promises to you will come true.

Narrator   Suddenly!

(All jump, God jumps off the chair)

Jacob awoke,

(Yawn)

And he was amazed and terrified.

(Shout 'Aagh!')

'God is really here in this place,' he cried, 'he hasn't forgotten me at all!'

(All look around amazed)

So he quickly built an altar.

(Two of the group bend over to form an altar)

And he worshipped the Lord there.

(Others kneel and say 'Amen!')

And he made a promise to God.

(Place hands on hearts)

'Lord,' he said, 'because you love me, and you've promised to stay with me – I will give you . . .

(Group hold up one finger and say 'One percent . . . ')

. . . of all you've given me.' Jacob was the last of the big spenders!

(Group turn away as if to leave, then stop and look up)

And the word of the Lord came to Jacob again – through his conscience saying:

(God climbs on the chair again)

God   Did I – the Sovereign Lord – promise you 1 percent of my love?

Narrator   And so Jacob thought again.

(All look as if they are thinking hard)

'Okay then,' he said, 'I was only joking. I'll give you . . . '

(All say 'Two percent' and hold up two fingers)

God   *(Wagging finger)*
                 Jacob!

Narrator   And Jacob finally got the message.

(All shout 'Ten percent!' holding both hands up)

                 At least! And so Jacob the grabber

('Gimme that!')

                 Became Jacob the giver.

(All shout 'Ten percent!' and hold up hands again)

                 And the Lord heard his prayers and honoured Jacob . . .

(All shout – 'One hundred percent!' – then all freeze)

Josh and the Wall

The account from Joshua chapter 6 of the battle of Jericho.

Cast   Narrator
             A group of four to eight people who respond with the
             appropriate words, noises and actions described in the
             brackets, and who include the following characters:
             God
             Member 1
             Member 2

*Begin with the group standing in a line facing away from the audience.
The narrator stands stage right, or off stage.*

Narrator   Back in the days when men were men.

(Group jump round, hold strong macho poses and grunt -- 'Ugh!')

             When ladies were ladies,

(Feminine poses, wolf whistles)

             And rabbits were rabbits,

(Rabbit noises and say 'Na . . . What'th up doc?')

             And walls didn't sell ice cream.

(Sing 'Just one cornetto')

             But instead, walls were huge, great things, thirty feet
             high, made of solid stone, and they were very, very . . .

(Group mime a wall, head butt it, then recoil and say 'Duh!')

             Thick! And no one could get over them.

(One leans on wall and says 'I just can't get over it!')

             See what I mean? Now Jericho was a city which was
             surrounded by a wall just like this.

(Group move into positions for next sequence)

             It was a very prosperous city, with lots of people buying
             and selling.

(One calls out 'Fresh fish, fresh fish – freshly fried fish')

             Which is very hard to say – as well as to sell!

*(In the following sequence the group create a rhythm of sound and
movements.)*

Subgroup 1   Fresh fish, fresh fish, get your fresh fish *(repeat)*

Subgroup 2   Special offer, special offer, going cheap this week *(repeat)*

Subgroup 3   Two for a pound or three for five *(repeat)*

Subgroup 4   Any old iron, any old iron, any, any, any old iron *(repeat)* Oi!

(And so on, adding any others. At the given signal – 'Oi!' – all freeze.)

Narrator   Now, the reason that Jericho had such big walls,

(All look up together, raising heads and placing hands above their eyes, then freeze.)

Was because no one was allowed to leave the city, or come into it – the gates were always kept locked.

(Two of the group form gates, and squeak shut with a loud 'Clang' which is echoed by all the group, who then rush to peer through the gates at the audience.)

Now one day, the Israelites were passing by, on their way to the promised land.

(All walk on the spot and sing -- 'Hi ho, hi ho, to Canaan we will go')

When the Lord stopped them, and gave them a message.

(God jumps onto a chair)

God   Er, I say, hello! This is the Lord here – I've got a jolly old message for you.

All   WHAT?
(They huddle around the one on the chair)

Narrator   And God told them that he wanted them to go and attack Jericho, because the people there didn't trust in God – they thought they were 'quite alright really' because they were protected by such big walls.

Member 1   But how will we get in?

God   Er . . . I know . . . you can knock the walls down!

All   *(Looking at audience)*
WHAT?

God   Don't worry – I've got a brilliant idea.

Member 2	So have I – let's give up and go home!
God	Exactly! I'll knock these walls down – not you. What you have to do is – trust me.
Narrator	And so God told the Israelites that all they had to do was get out their trumpets;

(Call along line 'Trumpets?' 'Trumpets!' 'Trumpets . . . ' They pass along a selection of whistles etc.)

March around the walls each day, and play them as loud as they could.

(Group march round in circles doing this)

Whether or not they could play in tune! And on the seventh day, they gave a final blast –

(Blast)

And an almighty shout . . .

All	Timber
Narrator	And . . .

(All sing ' . . . the walls came tumbling down.' Pause, look up. 'Aahh!' All scream and duck.)

And those huge, gigantic walls, which no one could possibly knock down – were completely . . .

All	FLATTENED *(All jump up and clap once)*
Narrator	By the hand of God.

(Shout 'Yea!' and punch the air, freeze with fists up)

And so, you see – it doesn't matter how big a problem may seem, or how impossible a job may be –
Listen to God,

All	Listen to God *(Shout and point to audience)*
Narrator	Do what he says,
All	Do what he says,
Narrator	Trust in him –
All	Trust in him –

Narrator   And he'll do the rest.

(Group don't repeat this line, instead shout 'Yea!' and punch the air. All freeze.)

Praying is Like Breathing

A simple sketch to illustrate the need to pray at all times, as recommended in 1 Thessalonians chapter 5 verse 17.

Cast   Narrator
A group of four to ten people who react to the reading

The group stand in a line.

Narrator   Praying is like breathing.

(Group all breathe, big movements)

It's old-fashioned but it works.
We need to breathe to stay alive,

(Alternate people stop breathing and collapse into next one's arms)

to continue growing,

(All watch an imaginary figure growing stage front)

and to achieve anything in life.

(Different poses of achievement)

It's recommended that one breathes steadily,

(Breathe together)

confidently,

(Freeze, with big smiles)

(Adds hastily)
and continuously;

(Breathe and smile)

believing in faith that, although one cannot see the air being inhaled, it is actually going in and out.

(Grit teeth, clench fists, big movements)

It would be unthinkable to attempt to survive without it.

(Puff out cheeks, pause, gasp for air)

Air is vital to our bodies, as prayer is to our spirits – we all need to breathe.

(Group freeze)

However, some have tried alternative methods.

For example, many people seem to think that by meeting together once a week and all breathing at the same time for one hour, they can then survive the rest of the week without the use of their lungs.

(All breathe in, one by one, then out, one by one)

Or, that all we need is twenty minutes breathing time at the beginning of each day, whilst still in a state of deep slumber.

(Pinch nose, look at watch, breathe quickly, fall asleep)

There are others for whom Wednesday night is their special breathing time, when they all have an evening of sharing air together in each other's homes.

(All form a group, breathe together, arms linked)

However, whilst many find these times of respiration beneficial, none is totally sufficient to keep us alive.

(Some breathe in line, some look at watch, some breathe in group)

In conclusion, on the maker's recommendations, we therefore advise that for best results one prays at all times, without ceasing. For those still not convinced, we recommend a simple test.

(Freeze)

Place one hand over the mouth,

(Hand over mouth)

the other over the nose,

(Pinch nose)

and do not remove until next Sunday morning.

(All freeze)

The Canaan Chorus

This is a simple sketch about the call of Abraham to step out into the unknown with God, and the way that he tried to run to Egypt when a famine hit Canaan. (See Genesis chapter 12).

Cast   Narrator
A chorus line of four to eight people

There are few stage directions, but a lot of verbal responses from the group. You may like to simplify this, or add other actions depending on the group performing it. The group should stand in a line facing the audience, one behind the other, so that only the first person in the line is visible. The narration has a sing-song feel to it.

Narrator   Once there was a man

Chorus   *(Lean or step outwards on alternate sides of the line, in a fan shape and shout)*
Called Abraham!

Narrator   He worked on a farm

Chorus   He worked on the land.
(They all point down)

Narrator   He had alot of crops

Chorus   Ooh arr! Ooh arr!

Narrator   And a lot of livestock

Chorus   Oink! Oink! Moo! Baa!

Narrator   Then one day God said to this man

Chorus   'Follow me old Abraham.
(Beckon with hand)

Narrator   Leave your cows and leave your crops,

Chorus   No more 'Neighbours' or 'Top of the Pops'.

Narrator   We're going together to a brand new land
Just bring your wife and follow my hand.'
So Abe set off with his nephew

Chorus   Lot!

Narrator   Though he was told to leave everything he'd got.
And soon they came to the land called

Chorus Canaan!
(Point stage left)

Narrator And there they worshipped God and

Chorus Praised him.
(Hands in praying position)

Narrator And things were going fine till the food ran out
And the whole of the land had a famine and a drought.

Chorus 'Quick! Let's go!'
(Point in the other direction)

Narrator Said Abraham.
And he packed his bags and off they ran
Down to Egypt, where they thought it would be nice,
And just to make sure Abe sold his wife.
'I know' he said,

Chorus 'Let's pretend you're my sister!'

Narrator He waved her goodbye – and he hadn't even kissed her.
When the people found out they really had snags
And Abe and his wife had to run and pack their bags.
They all went back to the land of

Chorus Canaan!
(Point)

Narrator And there they worshipped God and

Chorus Praised him.
(Praying hands)

Narrator So remember when you think that the going is tough
When you want to give up 'coz you think you've had enough.

Chorus Remember Abe and the trouble that he got
When he tried to run away with his nephew Lot.

(All freeze)

Prodigal Rap

A mime based on Luke chapter 15, the prodigal son.

Cast   Narrator

A group of two to six people who mime the actions printed in the brackets. Each movement should be frozen, presenting the audience with a series of 'photographs' to accompany the narration.

The group begin frozen as if in conversation.

Narrator   Now, a few years back there was a wise old man,

(One of group becomes the wise man, steps forward, pipe in mouth)

Lived on a ranch, had a clapped out van.

(All straighten hat. Drive van.)

Had two strong sons and life was swell,

(All strike he-man poses. Slap thighs, pantomime style.)

A hen, three gerbils and a wife as well.

(One becomes large wife, others cower)

But one fine day, working out in the rough,

(All dig)

The youngest boy said 'I've had enough!'

(Wipe sweat off brow)

So he dropped his spade on his brother's toe

(Throw down spade, hold foot in pain)

And he headed for his father just to let him know.

(All turn stage right, step once and freeze)

He packed his bags and he stood at the door.

(All pick up cases)

He said 'Diggin' ain't what my right arm's for.

(Raise right arm and drink)

Don't try to stop me 'cause I'm gonna go.

(Rub hands and step forward)

Gonna get me some fun – if you'll give me some dough?'
(Arrogantly slap back pocket and hold out hand for money)

It was a mean old day for the poor old man,
(One becomes father again. He wipes left eye, then right.)
'Cause he loved his son and couldn't understand
(Looks at others, shakes head and weeps)
Why he wanted to leave his family and home
(Father puts hand on another's shoulder. Others all shrug it off.)
But he gave him all his money and he watched him go.
(Father hands over money and waves goodbye. Others take it.)

Well, I'd be lying if I didn't tell you
(All tap side of nose, and point at audience knowingly)
He had a lot of fun – for a week or two.
(Wipe forehead and look awestruck)
Laughin' and dancin' and drinkin' home brew;
(Laugh, dance and drink)
The cars were fast and the girls were too.
(Drive sports car, girls drape over men)

Till one fine day he woke up in a daze,
(All stagger)
Smellin' worse than the neighbourhood strays.
(Smell armpits and wave hand in front of face)
His body was achin' and his brain was bad,
(Hold back and then head)
His friends had run off with everything he had.
(Pull out empty pockets)

Nobody cared now that he was broke.
(Try and attract attention of passing cars)
    His life had become a mighty bad joke.
(Kick the ground and shake head)
    Lost all he had and when he fell asleep
(Sleep on each other's shoulders)
    Someone stole the fillings from his two bad teeth.
(Yelp out loud and hold mouth in shock)

    Well, he felt pretty silly and he wandered around
(Walk on the spot looking bewildered)
    Till he got so thin that his pants fell down.
(Look down, realise and cover pelvis with arms)
    So he took a job dishing out pig swill
(Ladle out pig swill)
    And it smelt so bad that it made him ill.
(Hold stomach and vomit, mouth wide open)

    Then suddenly – he realised –
(Straighten up. Hold up one finger)
    What a fool he'd been – and he opened his eyes –
(Cover eyes with hand. Remove hand, eyes wide)
    He saw the waste – his life had become –
(Look down)
    He'd lost everything – for a week of fun.
(Dance, laugh, drink in slow motion – look unhappy)

    'I'll go on home,' he said that day –
(Look off stage)
    'I'll scrub the floors – for a servant's pay.
(Scrub floor)

What a fool – to reject my dad –

(Slap forehead)

Couldn't see just what I had.'

(Look down at empty hands)

Well, he walked on home in the midday sun.

(All turn and walk three steps on the spot)

It was the hardest thing he'd ever done.

(Wipe brow, face to audience)

He was a broken man now, nothing to lose,

(Stumble)

The holes in his life like the holes in his shoes.

(Hold up shoe, look at sole and wince)

He threw himself at the feet of his dad,

(Father turns back on the others. Others drop to knees.)

Said, 'Dad, I wasted everything I had.

(Stand. Recap on story -- drink, pigswill, vomit . . .)

I know I done wrong you should send me away –
But if I work for you will you let me stay?'

(Scrub floor. Drop to knees again and bow head.)

'Son, I love you,' the father replied.
'I thought you were lost, I figured you'd died.
It broke my heart when you went away
And I've been waiting for you to come home today.
I don't care where you've been or what you've done,
I just want you back, 'cause you're my son.'

(During these last lines, the father turns, jumps as he sees the others, rubs his eyes, then happily throws his arms in the air. One by one he helps the others to their feet, dusts them off and embraces them. All freeze.)

The Samaritan Rap

A rap based on the parable of the good Samaritan from Luke chapter 10.

Cast   One or more narrators who deliver the rap in the
appropriate style

You may like to use a vocal backing group to create the rhythm, or a drum machine.

Now, not long ago, once upon a time,
There were four young dudes in a bus queue line.
The first was a guy – a real cool cat,
Had his number sussed – knew just where he was at.
Trend was his name, the rat race his game,
His clothes all chic just to be the same.
He bought – what – he didn't need
Just to keep up with the other guy's greed.
He buys the things he don't need with the dough he don't have
To beat the folks he don't like just to have the last laugh.
What he wants – is – more and more,
He'll grab all you have as sure is sure.

The next guy in line weren't quite so bad,
Had his head in a book and his eyes in a fad –
He leered, looked, listened and learned;
But never got involved in case his fingers got burned.
He never did wrong, and smiled all the time;
Only drank milk and went to bed by nine.
I guess you could say: 'He's a real nice gent';
And though he did nothing it was surely well meant.

The third of the four – he was really bad news:
A man of the cloth from shoulders to shoes.
Went to meetings all day and he prayed all night -
Sang in the choir how to 'Fight the good fight'.
'cause he figured – that – it was best
Never to put the Lord your God to the test.
So he busied from dawn until Evensong,
Never stopped to think in case he got it wrong.

But it's the guy at the end that we're talking about:
He lived his own life, he didn't stomp, didn't shout.
Didn't like the others 'cause he counted 'em square;
And in church on a Sunday he was never there.

So there they were – all four – in a line
When a girl driving by hits a traffic sign!
They all caught the sound of the smash and the thud;
And they all turned around, saw the glass and the blood.
Now Mr Trend he saw his chance to help,
Saw the jewels and the bag and he helped himself.
Took the girl's wrist, not to check the pulse beat –
But to pocket her watch and make off down the street.

Mean – while, on the other side
They turned a blind eye coz the bus had arrived.
Mr Nice Gent he'd do what he could
But he wasn't trained right and he couldn't stand blood.
He'd phone the police – he'd call the old bill,
But he couldn't get close 'cause it might make him ill.
And the vicar agreed 'What a good idea!' –
To hop on board and just keep clear.
'cause the bus was late and about to go
And there were only two seats left in the back row.
And the vicar decreed that he didn't know
If they should get involved without the Lord's say-so.

But as the bus pulled out – they got a shock!
'cause the guy on the end was takin' stock.
He didn't have the training or the prayers to say
But he helped out the girl in his own good way.
He didn't seem to wait for a sign from above
And the blood and the glass didn't stop his love.
The vicar and his mate didn't know what to say
When they saw him take his wallet out and start to pay.
They thought 'love in action' was a TV show
And when they saw the girl recover it was quite a blow!

So, are – you – one of those guys?
Do you think that you know it? Do you think that you're wise?
Do you grab what you can; or hold on to what you got?
Or get involved when it hurts and risk losing the lot?
'cause a neighbour ain't a neighbour till he's giving away
So give it all that you've got and that's all you can say . . .
'cause a neighbour ain't a neighbour till he's giving away
So give it all that you've got and that's all you can say . . .

David and the Giant

The account from 1 Samuel chapter 17, the story we know as David and Goliath.

Cast   Narrator 1
Narrator 2
The giant
David

The two narrators tell the story, while David and the giant mime the action. Towards the end the giant does use dialogue when he grabs the script from one of the narrators. This piece requires enthusiasm and vigour!

Begin with the narrators standing stage right and left, with the giant asleep on a chair centre stage.

Narrator 1   Once upon a time there was a giant;

Narrator 2   A nice, gentle, peaceful giant.

(Giant sleeps on a chair)

Narrator 1   At least – he was nice, gentle and peaceful

Narrator 2   When he was asleep.

Narrator 1   Which he often was.

Narrator 2   But when he woke up . . .

(Narrator 2 sneezes, the giant wakes up)

Narrator 1   He wasn't nice, gentle or peaceful at all.

Narrator 2   In fact – he was downright horrible.

(Giant lumbers towards Narrator 2)

Narrator 1   And he did nasty things . . .

(Narrator 2 cowers in fear)

Narrator 2   Like twisting people's ears, stamping on their toes, and poking them in the eye . . . ow!

(Giant does all this to Narrator 2)

Narrator 1   And no one dared argue with him . . .

(Giant looks at the narrators who shake their heads)

Narrator 2   Because he was ten feet tall.

(Giant jumps on the chair to give himself extra height)

Narrator 1   Well, nearly anyway.

Narrator 2   And the reason he was so big . . .

Narrator 1   Was because he ate so much. He ate everything.

Narrator 2   Chips.

(The giant begins to empty his pockets and eat the contents)

Narrator 1   M & M's.

Narrator 2   Maltesers.

Narrator 1   Big Macs.

Narrator 2   Mars bars.

Narrator 1   All on the same plate.

Narrator 2   Anything and everything.

Narrator 1   In fact . . . all the things that are bad for you.

Narrator 2   YUK!

(Giant is not happy with this and jumps down off the chair)

Narrator 1   But if you tried to stop him he would . . .

(Giant approaches Narrator 2 with menace)

Narrator 2   Twist your ear, stamp on your toe, and poke your . . . ow!

(Giant does all this to Narrator 2)

Narrator 1   *(Enjoying this)*
He was horrible!

Narrator 2   *(Looking at Narrator 1)*
It's alright for you!

Narrator 1   *(Ignoring this)*
He didn't like people at all,

Narrator 2   *(Glaring at giant)*
And they didn't like HIM!

Narrator 1   Not only that . . .

(Giant stands on the chair and makes faces at the audience)

Narrator 2   But he didn't like God either,

(Giant looks up and makes faces at the ceiling)

Narrator 1   And he didn't put his trust in him.

Narrator 2   And that was his downfall.

(Narrator 2 sticks his tongue out at the giant. Giant sits down, a little unsure.)

Narrator 1   Now, in case you're wondering,

Narrator 2   This horrible giant's name was . . .

Narrator 1   Gladys.

(Giant threatens him)

Narrator 1   *(Hastily re-reading it)*
Goliath! Goliath!

Narrator 2   And one day he decided to join the army.

(Giant salutes)

Narrator 1   Because his army –

Narrator 2   The Philistines –

Narrator 1   Was fighting another army

(Giant marches up and down)

Narrator 2   Called the Israelites.

Narrator 1   And while the Israelites were nice people . . .

Narrator 2   Who didn't eat Big Macs, M&M's and chips . . .

(Giant sits and begins to fall asleep)

Narrator 1   The Philistines were just like Goliath:

Narrator 2   *(Said with feeling)*
Horrible!

Narrator 1   Except when they were asleep.

(Giant is now asleep)

Narrator 2   *(Seeing Giant)*
Whatever you do – please, nobody sneeze.

(Narrator 2 then suddenly sneezes. Giant wakes up.)

Narrator 2   *(Hastily continuing)*
Now one day, while Goliath was asleep . . .

(Giant hesitates, thinks, then goes back to sleep)

Narrator 1   The Israelites sent along their secret weapon to get rid of him.

Narrator 2   And their fantastic secret weapon . . .

Narrator 1 (*Reading incredulously*)
Was three feet two inches tall?

Narrator 2 In fact – he was just a little boy

Narrator 1 Called David.

Narrator 2 But he was very brave.

(*Enter David, wearing school cap and shorts. He tiptoes over to the giant and knocks on an imaginary door. The giant doesn't wake. He knocks again. Still no response. Just then Narrator 2 sneezes. The giant wakes instantly. David meanwhile is now looking at Narrator 2 to see why he sneezed. He knocks again, but now the giant has opened the door and David's fist knocks on his chest. David looks up at the giant, then jumps back. The giant grabs him by the shoulder.*)

Narrator 1 (*Deep voice*)
'Yes!' said the giant,

Narrator 2 (*Also deep voice*)
'And what do you want?'

(*David smiles sweetly up at the giant*)

Narrator 1 And in spite of the fact that David was only three foot two . . .

Narrator 2 And the giant was ten foot tall . . .

(*David looks at the giant from head to foot*)

Narrator 1 David wasn't afraid.

(*David and the giant look at the narrators, amazed*)

Narrator 2 Because he trusted in God.

(*Narrator 2 points up, David nods, the giant scoffs. David steps back and pulls himself up to his full height. Then he smiles sweetly and sidles up to the giant again. He beckons.*)

Narrator 1 'Er, Goliath?'

Narrator 2 Said David.

Narrator 1 'What?'

Narrator 2 Said Goliath.

(*The giant steps close to David and leans towards him. David then twists his ear, stamps on his toe, and pokes him in the eye.*)

Narrator 1   *(In time with the giant who mouths the 'Ow!'s)*
'Ow! Ow!' and 'Ow!'

Narrator 2   Said the giant.

Narrator 1   Or words to that effect.

Narrator 2   *(With enthusiasm)*
But the giant quickly recovered, ran at David, and completely flattened him!

(Giant begins to do this, then stops. Both Giant and David look in horror at Narrator 2.)

Giant   What!

Narrator 2   *(Frightened)*
That's what it says here!

Giant   But that's not right.

Narrator 1   Said the giant.

Giant   *(He grabs the script and looks at it)*
It should say 'David took out his sling, put in a stone, swung it round his head . . .'

(David follows all these instructions)

Giant   'And hit Goliath with it!'

(The giant looks up, and realises. He turns to David, who swings the sling and fires it. The giant recoils and collapses.)

Narrator 2   That fooled him!

Narrator 1   Said the narrator.

Narrator 2   And the giant thudded to the ground.

(When the giant hears this he hastily gets up again, staggers, and dies.)

Narrator 1   THUD!

Narrator 2   Never to be seen again.

Narrator 1   Yippee!

(Narrator 1 and Narrator 2 throw their scripts in the air. David dusts his hands.)

Narrator 2   Er, but just in case . . . please – nobody sneeze.

(David acts as if he is about to, but then stifles it. Narrator 2 then sneezes. The others look horrified. The giant stays dead. All freeze.)

And Now for the Bad News . . .

This sketch is taken from the account in 2 Chronicles chapter 20 of how King Jehoshaphat defeated his enemies, not by his own strategy but by listening to God and obeying him: an unusual story, which highlights the power of prayer.

Cast   Jehoshaphat
Four reluctant messengers (One, Two, Three and Four)

The piece begins with the King seated, reading his newspaper. Cautiously the messengers shuffle in, talking amongst themselves.

One   You tell him.

Two   What!

One   You tell him.

Two   No, no. You're actually much better qualified.

One   Me? But what difference does a GCSE in woodwork make?

(In spite of his protests, One is pushed forward)

One   Ahem. King Jehoshaphat.

(All bow. King nods.)

Good to see you, how are you?

Jehoshaphat Not too good actually, a little under the weather.

One   Good, goo . . . what?
(To the others)
He's feeling a bit under the weather.

Three   So?

One   So this could finish him off.

Four   He's only got a cold.

One   No, too risky.

Four   Too risky?

One   The shock could give him flu!

Jehoshaphat Ahem, you were going to say something?

One   Me? No, no, no . . .

Two   Yes, he was.

One	What? Oh, well, he's right. I'm afraid that I have to tell you that . . . that he's got some bad news for you. *(Indicates Two)*
Two	Me?
One	Yes, tell the King.
Three	Go on then.
Two	Ah . . . you mean the bad news about him? *(Points to Three)* Actually, I think you should tell him yourself.
Three	What? Oh dear, I seem to be losing my [voice] . . . *(He mouths the last word)*
Four	*(Sighs)* Alright, I'll tell him. We've got some bad news, sir.
Three	Very bad news.
Four	I thought you'd lost your voice?
Three	Oh! [I have.] *(He mouths these last words)*
Four	Well, anyway, it is quite bad.
Two	Heart breaking.
One	Tragic.
Two	Suicidal.
Four	Well, let's just say – it's not good.
Three	Not good? It's flippin' awful!
Four	You'll lose more than your voice in a minute!
Jehoshaphat	Perhaps I should be the judge of the situation?
Two	Good idea.
One	Excellent idea, King. He'll tell you the terrible, abysmal, catastrophic news – and you can be the judge.
Four	Shhh! It's about our enemies, Sir.
One	Yes, you know – the really brutal, nasty ones.
Four	Shut up! Now, I'd sit down if I were you. Oh you are, right. Now, about our enemies, they . . . a cup of tea, perhaps?

Two	Break it to him gently.
One	Yes. Tactfully.
Three	VERY.
Four	Yes, alright, I will. Jehoshaphat – a colossal army has just invaded us and they're about to wipe us out completely. *(The other three faint)*
Four	There. *(Turning to others)* Was that okay . . . oh!
Jehoshaphat	*(Calmly folds his paper)* Oh, that's very serious.
Four	Yes, I thought you'd be devastated, Sir. I'll go and draw up the conditions of our surrender.
Jehoshaphat	*(Nodding thoughtfully)* No.
Four	Better to give in peacefully than lose . . . I beg your pardon?
Jehoshaphat	We must pray.
Four	Oh! Oh, alright. *(He bows his head to do so)*
Jehoshaphat	*(Deep in thought)* Call the people together.
Four	*(Thinking this is part of the prayer)* Mmm.
Jehoshaphat	Then we shall pray.
Four	Mmm. What? Oh, I see, I thought you meant . . .
Jehoshaphat	We must pray; seek the Lord; fast.
Four	The quicker the better, Sir.

(Jehoshaphat gets up to leave)

Four	Where are you going?
Jehoshaphat	To pray with the people.
Four	But . . . this could be dangerous . . . couldn't we surrender first . . . just a little bit?

(Jehoshaphat and Four exit. Other three wake up gradually. Four re-enters with a scroll.)

Four   Amazing.

Three   Is it all over?

Four   Yes.

(All shake heads sadly)

Two   Was it painful?

Four   Not really.

One   Tell us about the . . .

Four   Fast?

One   Any speed you like.

Four   No. We fasted and prayed together, the whole nation – before going out to fight them.

Two   Fight them?

Three   How many casualties?

Four   Ooh, thousands!

(All shake heads again)

Three   I knew we shouldn't have told him when he had a cold!

Four   No. Not our casualties. Theirs. Before we went out, the Lord spoke to us. He said the battle was his – not ours. All we had to do was trust him, and praise him. He took care of the rest.

Two   You mean . . . we won?

Four   Yes. Well, no. He won. We didn't even get to fight. The Lord fought for us. Look, this was his promise:
(Reads from a scroll)
'You won't have to fight this battle, just take up your positions and wait, you'll see the Lord give you victory.'

Three   Incredible.

One   Well, what did I tell you?

Two   'Give in' – that's what you told us.

Three   So, the Lord really will fight our battles, amazing.

Two   The King must be over the moon. How is he?

Four   Actually . . .
              (Pause)
              he's in bed with flu!

(All freeze)

Elisha and the Oil

The story in 2 Kings chapter 4 where Elisha helps a poor widow and, with God's help, performs a miracle.

Cast   Elisha
            Widow
            Two sons (1 and 2)

The scene takes place outside the widow's house. Elisha enters and mops his brow.

Elisha   Oh dear. Oh dearie, dearie, dear.
(He wipes his brow)
It's hard being an old testament prophet, you know. So many messages from God to announce. So many kings to tell off. So many miracles . . . I think I'll just sit here and have a nice snooze.

(He lies down. Enter Widow, in a hurry. She trips over him.)
Ow!

Widow   Sorry. But I'm in a hurry.

Elisha   What's the problem?

Widow   It's awful, I'm just a poor old widow, with three sons to feed . . .

(Son 1 and Son 2 enter)

Sons   TWO sons mother. You've only got TWO sons! And a bad memory!
(They exit again)

Widow   *(Counting on her fingers)*
Oh dear. Adding up never was my strong point! What comes after one? You should know *(To Elisha)* – you're a prophet!

Elisha   Two! Now listen, my name's Elisha.

Widow   That's a funny name!

Elisha   Well, at least I can count! And I can also help you.

Widow   Oh could you? We have no food at home. And I've got three sons to feed . . .

Elisha   Two sons – you've got TWO sons.

Widow   Gosh! That's clever how did you know – you must be a prophet! But what can I do? All I have is one small jar of olive oil.

Elisha   Right. Get that jar of oil, and bring it here.

Widow   I'll just call my sons – John! And John! And John! They're all called John: it's easier to remember that way.

(Enter Son 1 and Son 2)

Elisha   Right. Let's find that jar of olive oil.

(They all run in the same direction, collide, then run again, and collide again. After that panic breaks out and they run everywhere, searching for the jar.)

Son 2   Got it!

(Everyone stops)

               Oh sorry, this isn't it – it's my aftershave . . .

(They all run again)

Son 1   Got it.
               (He holds up a small bottle)

(Widow runs past and grabs it)

Widow   I'll have that!

Son 2   No! I want it.
               (He leap-frogs over her, and takes the bottle)

(Elisha trips him up, the bottle is thrown up in the air, and Elisha catches it.)

Son 1   That was cool.

Elisha   Yes, but I am a prophet! Now, get all the pots and pans in the house, anything that will hold water.

Son 2   How about the bath?

(They each bring a pot, or a bucket. Son 1 brings a sieve.)

Widow   That's no good!

Son 1   But it's only got a few holes in the bottom!

Elisha   Now for the good bit. Let's talk to God and ask for his help. Because we need a miracle here.

(They all stop and bow their heads and pray silently.)

Elisha	Right!
	(He claps his hands and the others jump)
	Start pouring that little bottle into all these.
Widow	Wait. We're not all here – there's only two of my sons . . .
Son 1	Mother, be quiet and pour!

(She tips the bottle into each container. They look amazed.)

Son 2	Wow! Amazing, it's filling all the buckets. It's just pouring, and pouring and pouring!
Widow	Quick, bring another bucket.
Son 1	No more left – you've filled everything in the house!
Widow	Gosh – it's stopped now, just in time.
Elisha	There you are – now sell all this oil, and you'll have enough money to pay your debts and support your family!
Son 1	How did you do this?
Elisha	It wasn't me – it was God. Nothing is impossible for him. I trusted him, and he did a miracle for you. So remember, keep talking to him.
Sons	Wow!
Widow	Me and my three sons will never be able to thank you!
Elisha	You're right about that! Byee . . .

(Elisha exits)

Jonah and the Whale

A sketch based on the book of Jonah.

Cast   Narrator
        Jonah
        The whale
        Boatman

OR   A narrator and a chorus of four to six people who all
        become Jonah, the boatman, the boat, the whale's mouth
        and the people of Ninevah

*As you can see from the above list of characters, this sketch may either
be performed by a chorus of actors, or with each character cast
separately.*

*Either way, this sketch needs to be presented with vigour, and props
and costume may also be used. Jonah may be portrayed as a broad
Yorkshireman.*

Narrator   Once there was a whale

(Enter one person wailing; or the chorus wail)

        Not that kind of wail – a big fish.

(Enter a person swimming around, opening mouth, goldfish style)

        And there was a man, called Jonah –

(Enter Jonah or one of the chorus, running on the spot)

        Why are you running, Jonah?

Jonah   *(Looks cautiously around)*
        Well don't tell anyone, but I'm running away from God!

Narrator   You see, God had told Jonah to go to Ninevah. But Jonah
        didn't want to – so he decided to run away.

Jonah   Oi! I told you not to tell anyone!

Narrator   Well, he wasn't getting very far . . . but people never do
        when they run away from God.

Jonah   I know, I need a boat.

(Enter the boatman, or the chorus become the boat)

Narrator   And so Jonah got on board.

Jonah   We're not getting very far.

Boatman/ Boat	Shouldn't we have a sail?
Jonah	Good idea! I'll get someone to buy my clothes – then I can get a disguise, and hide from God.
Boatman/ Boat	No, a sail – not a sale!

(Enter the whale)

Whale	Did someone say whale?
Narrator	No. A sail, not a whale.
Whale	Oh well, too late now. I'd better swallow Jonah anyway, while I'm here.
Jonah	That's a bit unfair.
Whale	I know, he tastes horrible – yuk!
Narrator	And so God made the whale swallow Jonah, to stop him from running away.

(Chorus change from boat to form a huge mouth. Jonah falls through the mouth, and sits there – looking disgruntled.)

Whale/ Chorus	Chomp, chomp, chomp. Tasty, tasty, very, very tasty; he's very tasty!
Narrator	And for three days Jonah was stuck in the fish.
Whale	I think I've got indigestion!
Jonah	I think I'm in a mess!
Boatman/ Chorus	I think I don't understand this story!
Narrator	Well, you see Jonah was running away from God . . .
Jonah	*(Sticking his head out of the mouth)* I told you not to tell anyone!
Whale/ Chorus	Chomp, chomp, chomp!

(As Jonah withdraws his head)

Narrator	Sorry. Anyway, God wanted Jonah in a place called Ninevah, which just happened to be where the whale was going.

Whale	I think I'm going to be sick!
Jonah	Good. 'Coz it smells awful in here, and I wish I'd never run away.
Narrator	Jonah said he was sorry to God . . .
Jonah	Sorry.
Narrator	. . . and the whale spewed him out onto the beach.
Whale/ Chorus	Blugh!

(Jonah rolls out of the whale's mouth)

Narrator	*(With distaste)* Thank you!
Whale	That's my favourite bit!
Narrator	Yes, well you can go now. And Jonah found himself on the beach.
Jonah	Ooh good, I think I'll have a sunbathe!
Narrator	No you don't – God has a job for you, Jonah!
Jonah	I told you not to tell . . . Oh, alright then. Come here you lot and listen to this. *(Jonah mimes preaching to the rest of the chorus; or to the audience)*
Narrator	And so Jonah told all the people there about God – and they all put their trust in him.
Jonah	Can I go home now?
Whale	Can I have an indigestion tablet?
Boatman/ Chorus	Can someone please explain this story to me?
Narrator	Well, Jonah was running away from God . . .
Jonah	I told you not to tell anyone!
Narrator	Sorry . . . but we'll keep it a secret – *(Turns to audience)* Won't we?

(All freeze)

Nativity Scene

Not surprisingly, this is a Christmas sketch, and one that looks at the materialism that so often dominates the 'festive season'. It is fairly lighthearted, but begins to point us to the reality of Christmas, and a Saviour who will return one day.

Cast   Action Man
         Master of the Universe (Master)

The two characters are dolls dressed in typical nativity costume. They are part of a nativity tableau and are both rather fed up . . .

The scene is set in the home of a young boy called Dougal, late on Christmas day.

Master   'Ere, can we move yet?

Action Man   I'm not sure, have all them people gone?

Master   *(Looks cautiously round)*
         Yea.
         (Sighs)

(They relax their rigid positions)

         Thank goodness for that. These nativity scenes are hard work.

Action Man   Plastic baby again I see.

Master   Well, you can talk, what were you before a shepherd – a Sindy doll?

Action Man   Action Man actually – if you must know.

Master   *(Peeping inside Action Man's shirt)*
         Ooh! Have you got one of them little cords that you pull to . . .

(Pulls out a string. Action Man slaps his hand.)

Action Man   Yes, I have, if it's any business of yours. Anyway, what are   you normally? I mean, when you're not posing as Mary . . .

Master   Mary! I'm a wise man, mate.

Action Man   Cor, they must be scraping the barrel. Well, what's your normal job?

Master   Oh, I don't like to brag.

Action Man Oh go on, tell me.

Master Well . . . I'm really – a Master of the Universe!

Action Man Get out! You haven't got the body.

Master It's not all physique ya know.

Action Man Huh, try telling that to Frank Bruno.

Master It's mental power,
(Taps his temple)
psychopathic.

Action Man You can say that again! This must be a bit of a let down, then – from mastering the universe to standing in camel's dung.

Master They bought little Dougal a mountain bike for Christmas, he doesn't want to know me anymore.

Action Man I know what you feel like. I was replaced by a pregnant gerbil.

Master Every Christmas it's the same – more clothes, more toys, more food, more drink.

Action Man And every Boxing Day it's the same – all leftovers and hangovers.

Master It's like they're addicted to it.

Action Man No – it's more than that. I reckon it's part of their religion.

Master Eh?

Action Man I heard two of them talking – it's a sort of annual creed. Every year they recite it: *he* says 'I believe it's gonna be another expensive year.' To which *she* replies 'I trust you'll stay sober this time.' This is usually followed with the response 'I can't believe the price of that whisky in Safeways.' Then comes a real giveaway 'Heaven knows what we're gonna buy the kids.' And he then remarks that God knows as well. You see – it's all a religous ceremony.
These humans are crazy.
(Pause)
D'ya think he was ever real – that baby?

Master   Well, he's been plastic as long as I've been standing here.

Action Man No, I mean in reality.

Master   Oh yea, a long time ago – when he was first born. It was all very real then. Christmas was a vital event. It involved priests and kings, and soldiers and angels, the sins of the world – and a very frightened young mother.

Action Man And now?

Master   Now? Well, if you look carefully into it – you can see a King who's gonna come back one day, and reign forever. But for most people it's just . . . plastic – like that baby.

Action Man And like us.

Master   You speak for yourself – I'm a Master of the Universe.

Action Man Really? Well you'd better watch out, coz it looks very much like young Dougal's about to leave his bubblegum all over you.

Master   WHAT?

(Both freeze looking up in horror.)

No Room . . .

Another Christmas sketch! This time looking at our attitudes to the amount of time and preperation we put in to 'get it right'.

Cast   Angel
Girl
Two men (Man 1 and Man 2)
Four People (Persons 1-3 can be of either sex, but Person 4 should be female, and act as a rather snooty, older lady)
Any number of 'extras' who decorate and clean the Church

The scene is a church, very early one Christmas Eve morning. The lights are dim, and the sound of a carol is heard in the background. A dishevelled angel enters cautiously, when he realises that no one else is around he relaxes and begins to talk to himself. The carol fades out.

Angel   Brilliant. Absolutely brilliant. I'm sent here on a special mission to alert the world, and what happens – the world's still in bed. Marvellous, flippin' humans they really make me s . . .
(He suddenly notices the audience)
Ah. Hello. I was just thinking about you lot. I don't suppose you've seen the congregation of this church? No, I didn't think so, I suppose it is a little on the early side. 'While mortals sleep the angels keep their watch of wondering . . . er, something or other.' Never could remember them carols, that's why they chucked me out of the choir, just because I happened to announce 'Glory to God in the Forest' when we met them shepherds. Anyway, just time to take the weight off my halo for a few minutes . . .

(As the angel takes a seat and drifts off to sleep, Man 1, Man 2 and the 'extras' enter the scene, they mime cleaning, decorating, chatting. Occasionally they notice the angel and look him up and down. Music begins again in the background. After a few minutes the Angel wakes.)

Angel   Ahhh . . .
(He yawns loudly, then jumps as he sees Man 1 peering down at him)
AHHH!

Man 1   Who are you?

Angel   *(Suddenly remembering)*
               Ah well, I, ahem, I am an angel.
               (Polishes his halo)
               And I have an import . . .

(Before he can finish the man hastily slinks away, looking horrified)

Angel   Er, I say – I said I'm an . . . and I've . . . oh dear.

(He scratches his head and turns to see a rubber plant thrust in his arms by Man 2)

Man 2   Hold this will ya, guv?

Angel   Oh,right. I'm an angel, by the way.

Man 2   *(Stares at him)*
               You're a what?

Angel   *(Suddenly losing his nerve, and covering his halo with a nearby hat)*
               Oh, nothing. Actually, I'm looking for a place where a friend of mine might be welcome.

Man 2   D'you know what time of year it is? Christmas. You'll be lucky to sleep in a barn at this time of year.

Angel   Funny you should mention that. Because he did once, sleep in a barn, I mean.

Man 2   Who?

Angel   Jesus.

Man 2   I know that. That's what we happen to be celebrating. We don't decorate this place for pleasure ya know. It's Christmas – we have to.

Angel   You know the story then.

Man 2   What? Of them daft angels – singing in the highest. And the wise men and the pig farmers.

Angel   Pig farmers?

Man 2   I know that old story mate.

Angel   Shepherds. Not pig farmers. We're talking about the Jews here. And what do you mean – daft angels?

(However, the man has wandered off, leaving his rubber plant)

(The angel moves to different 'extras' to talk to them, but he is shoved, ignored and used as a dumping ground. Eventually frustration overcomes him.)

Angel   STOP!

(Everyone does so, and looks at him)

Oh, er thank you. Now . . .

Person 1   Who are you?

Angel   I'm an . . .
(Goes to remove his hat, then thinks better of it)
I'm a messenger. And a friend of mine is coming . . .

Person 2   A friend of yours?

Person 3   Who?

Angel   Well . . .

Person 4   You're not one of them Jehovah's Witnesses are you?

Angel   Madam, certainly not.

Person 1   Jeremy Beadle. You're off the TV.

(Others echo this idea)

Angel   PLEASE! Listen. You're probably aware that this is a significant time of year.

Person 2   Yea, I'm significantly broke.

Angel   As I was saying – this is an expensive . . . I mean a significant time, when we celebrate Jesus coming to earth. However, be encouraged, I have some good news for you . . .

Person 3   Are you insinuating that Jesus coming to earth was bad news?

Person 4   Young man, have you been washed in the blood?

Angel   There'll be plenty of blood in a minute, dear, if you don't let me finish.

Person 2   *(Looking off-stage)*
Ooh vicar, come and listen to this!

Angel   Listen – Jesus is coming back again. And I've been asked to let you know.

Person 1	We know he's coming back.
Angel	NOW!
Persons 1-4	NOW?
Angel	Yes. Rather appropriate time of year, we thought. Now when he arrives there's certain jobs need doing.
Person 1	Ooh, I'll help.
Person 4	He can have Christmas dinner with us.
Person 3	Hey, I've got a great present he can have.
Person 2	We'll give him supper.
Angel	No.
Persons 1-4	No?
Angel	No.
	(Opens a scroll)
	These are the jobs he wants doing:
	(Reads)
	Help for praying with the sick. Food and money to give away. Prison visits to be arranged. A tour of the red light district. And plenty of children.

(Stunned silence)

Person 3	That's not very Christmassy.
Angel	Oh, and the important bit – could you all spare a few hours tomorrow morning for a get together here, so we can all chat and have a good time together. Only he'd love to get to know you all better.
Person 1	A few hours?
Person 4	What about the lunch?
Person 2	We know him, already.
Person 3	I've got the Carol Service to prepare.
Person 4	What about the Queen's speech – he surely doesn't want us to miss that.
Person 1	Yea, and the presents round the tree – and Trivial Persuasion.
Person 4	Pursuit!

52

Angel	Now, I'll just stick this list up here, on the wall, so you can all sign up for the appropriate jobs. Then when he comes . . . *(He turns to see they have all slipped off)* . . . he'd love to meet you all. Oh!

(One scruffy little girl steps forward)

Girl	'Ere, mister. Did you say God's coming to visit?
Angel	*(Sadly)* Yes.
Girl	Jesus? When, soon?
Angel	Very soon. Maybe even tomorrow.
Girl	*(Cautiously)* You're the angel Gabriel aren't you?
Angel	Nearly – my name's Andrew actually. But Gabriel taught me to fly.
Girl	Wow! Is that why all them posh folks have scarpered? To get ready to meet God?
Angel	Well, sort of. Not exactly. They're all a bit busy – thinking about his birthday. But hopefully they'll have time to come and see him.
Girl	Oh well, don't worry, mister, I will. I love Jesus. I'll come and see him. I'm gonna wait here for him – you tell him when you see him.
Angel	Haven't you got things to do?
Girl	No. I can't afford it. I ain't rich like them. 'Ere, when you see him, tell him I got a pressie for him an' all. Look! *(She pulls a tattered paper from her pocket)*
Girl	It's a picture of him. My dad give it me – just before he run off. D'ya think Jesus'll like it?
Angel	I think he'll love it. And you know, you're wrong about those other people – you're the one that's rich. See ya soon.
Girl	'Bye.

(He leaves her holding the crumpled picture. Freeze.)

The Best Attitudes

Taken from Matthew chapter 5.

Cast   Narrator
A group of two to eight adults or children who respond to the narration

This piece relies upon simple but strong movements and words, and the group acting must freeze their positions each time they move.

Begin with the group standing side by side, facing away from the audience and leaning on one another.

Narrator   One day, Jesus sat down on a hill and began to talk to everyone.

(The group swivel round and lean into a sitting position, back to back. They each rest their chin on their hand.)

He said to them: If you want to be happy,

(Group throw back their heads and laugh loudly)

If you want to be satisfied,

(They stand, lean on each other and pat stomach. Say 'Ah!')

If you want to be fulfilled,

(Some mime eating noisily, others slurp drinks)

And at peace.

(Place heads on each others' shoulders. Snore loudly.)

Then you can be.

(They wake up, look at the narrator and say hopefully: 'Really?')

Sure. Just follow me – and do this –

(They jump to face left and take one big step)

Admit you need God;

(Kneel side by side. In twos, the person on the right places their left hand beside the other one's right hand so that they form cupped hands together. They then look up.)

Cry for the world;

(Still in twos, the person on the right bows their head in their hands. The person on the left looks up in anguish and shouts 'Help!')

Show love,

(They comfort one another)

Be obedient,

(All stand, salute. Say 'Yep!')

Seek God,

(They search high and low, peering round one another)

And work for peace.

(They embrace one another)

So, if you want happiness –

(Group look sad, bored, depressed)

Don't seek it . . .

(Group look at the narrator)

Look for God instead . . .

(They all turn and look up abruptly. All freeze.)

The Healing of the Lame Man

As the title suggests, this sketch is based on Jesus' healing of the paralysed man from Luke chapter 5. It is a fairly lighthearted sketch, and the climax should be one of celebration as the healing is discovered.

Cast   Man
            Four friends (One, Two, Three and Four)

The four friends enter carrying the Man on a stretcher. The Man is complaining and struggling to get away.

Four   Get back on that stretcher.

Man   I don't feel too ill actually.

Three   Course you do, now lie down.

Man   But honestly – I feel fine . . .

Two   Well, you look a funny colour to me.

Man   What!

One   Look, of course you're not well – you haven't walked for twenty-three years.

Man   Well . . . that is true, but . . .

Two   I mean, just look at his eyes, and feel that temperature!

Man   What do you mean? Oh listen, please, will you put me down?

(They have now reached centre stage)

            I don't want to . . . stop it . . . let me go . . . HELP! HELP! I'm being pushed into this . . .

One   Oh be quiet. It's for your own good.

Two   Of course you want to see Jesus. I mean - who wouldn't?

Man   ME!

Four   Oh . . . stop complaining.

(The four friends turn and look off stage)

Three   Hey, the door's far too narrow. We'll never get him through. And all those people!

Man   What? Oh dear, what a shame, and I was so looking forward to it. Still . . . can't win 'em all.

(However, his friends aren't listening, but looking upwards and offstage.)

Man	Hey, what are you planning now?
One	The roof.
Man	THE ROOF!
One	The roof.
Four	Good idea.
Man	What do you mean – 'good idea'? It's an extremely dangerous idea.
Three	If we just remove a few tiles, and that beam . . .
Man	*(Sitting upright)* Now listen, who's gonna pay for all this damage?
Four	We'll all pay.
Man	Who asked you?
Two	Agreed. We'll all pay.
Man	I won't.
Three	Then we will.
Man	You're mad.
Two	And you're gonna be healed.
Man	I might not want to be.

(Friends pause. They sigh and give up the argument.)

Three	Oh alright. You win. Come on, let's go, lads.

(They place him on the floor and turn and walk away, leaving the man stranded on the stretcher.)

Man	*(Realising his problem)* Ah! Well, on the other hand . . .

(They run back. Pick him up and rush him off stage in the direction of the roof. They quickly re-enter, without the man, staring eagerly off stage.)

Four	What did Jesus say?
One	*(Disappointed)* He said his sins are forgiven.

Two	But . . . he can't say that. That's not fair.
Three	*(To Two)* You said he was going to be healed, not forgiven.
Two	Don't blame me, I didn't know he'd been sinning, did I?
Four	Wait a minute, let's all keep cool. I still believe he'll be healed, don't you?
Two	Well . . . I suppose so.
One	I do. Of course Jesus will heal him.

(They turn and stare at Three)

Three	*(Awkwardly)* What are you looking at me for? Alright, I believe it too . . . I think.
One	*(Looking off stage)* Hey, he's gone. And where's Jesus?
Three	That's great. Forgives his sins, and off he goes . . .

(As they stand staring off, the man enters from the other side of the stage and joins the line of them.)

Man	Hello, what are you lot doing? *(Trying to see off stage)*
Two	We're looking for . . . *(At this point he turns and sees him)* Oh!
Three	*(Looking round)* What . . . AHH! It's you!

(Three falls into the arms of One, who lowers him to the floor and steps over him to get to the man.)

Four	He's been healed.
One	Amazing! Praise God! A miracle!
One, Two, Three and Four	Look, he can walk . . . It's a miracle . . . Jesus did this . . . Praise God . . .

(All freeze, praising God and celebrating.)

Good Friday

A sketch about the nature of Good Friday; the sadness of Jesus' death, and the hope of the Resurrection.

Cast   Jemima
              Teacher

The teacher is a fairly brisk Sunday school type. Jemima is a rather spoilt little girl. The scene is the church, before the class begins.

The teacher marches Jemima into the class and gives her a couple of old leaves.

Teacher   Now, Jemima, take these leaves and go and stand in the middle over there.

(She hands the leaves over. Jemima takes them and glares at them.)

Jemima   Why?

Teacher   Because you're a tree Jemima.

Jemima   No, I'm not!

Teacher   Yes you are. In today's story you are. Go and stand over there.

Jemima   Don't want to.

Teacher   Yes you do.

(She marches Jemima over, Jemima is very reluctant. The teacher leaves her and steps away.)

    Put the leaves up higher, dear.

(Jemima shoves them in her mouth)

Teacher   Not there – hold them up.

(Jemima aggressively shoves them in the air in her clenched fists)

Teacher   Not that way.

(Jemima turns her fists upside down)

Teacher   *(Sighs and walks back, trying to be patient)*
    Like a tree dear.

(She pulls Jemima into a tree-like position. Jemima stands scowling.)

    And smile dear.

Jemima   Trees don't smile.

Teacher	Yes they do!
Jemima	No they don't!
Teacher	*(Gritted teeth)* This one does!
Jemima	No it doesn't . . .
Teacher	JEMIMA!

(Miraculously Jemima puts on a huge smile)

Jemima	*(Through the smile)* What's it for anyway, this stupid tree?
Teacher	It's not stupid – it's for our Good Friday story.
Jemima	What's good about it?
Teacher	It's the day Jesus died.
Jemima	But that's not good . . .
Teacher	Yes it is.

(Jemima looks at the teacher, then turns and marches away)

Jemima	I'm telling my mum that you said it's good that Jesus is dead.
Teacher	*(Marching her back)* Jemima! Stand there – what's wrong with you?
Jemima	Well, I don't want to be a tree, and I don't think I like Good Friday.
Teacher	Why not?
Jemima	It's awful. It's sad, and horrible and boring.
Teacher	*(Softening)* No it isn't – that's why it's called *Good* Friday – because Jesus dying on the cross means that you and I can be forgiven for things we do wrong. And that's good news.
Jemima	But we can never enjoy ourselves on Good Friday, can we?
Teacher	Well, we do spend time thinking about all that Jesus went through for us – and when he died on the cross it did hurt him a lot. But three days later he rose from the

dead again – and that's something we can look forward to.

(Jemima thinks about this and takes up the tree position. The teacher turns away.)

Jemima *(Dropping the position again)*
So does that mean we can enjoy ourselves on Good Friday or not?

Teacher Yes – you can. After all, Jesus is alive now, we're just remembering his death 2000 years ago – he's alive really. But remembering sometimes makes us sad. Okay?

Jemima One more question? Have I absolutely got to be a tree?

Teacher *(Walks over to her)*
No. There's also a pig in our story.

Jemima *(Quickly takes up the position again)*
I'll be a tree . . .

(Freeze)

The Gospel Truth

A lively piece of drama which describes Jesus' life and ministry.

Cast   Boy
             Girl

This sketch is rather slapstick in style, involving several custard pies. The boy and the girl should be acted by adults, or very competent children. The slap on the following page should be carefully staged -- the boy clapping his hands to create the right sound as the girl pretends to hit him. It takes place somewhere outdoors . . .

The boy enters looking disgruntled.

Boy   Oh, I'm fed up. I'm bored. I've got nothing to do. Mum's chucked me out of the house so that she can tidy up – yuk! That means my bedroom will be in a right state when I get back. It'll be awful. Everything will be 'organised' and I won't be able to find a thing. All my stuff will be tucked neatly away – hidden in drawers and cupboards – it'll take me ages to get it all out and put it on the carpet again. I hate things being tidy. It's much better when everything's thrown on the floor and . . . 'ullo?
(He sees a custard pie)
What's this then? Hey! This is great! A custard pie – I could make a right mess with this. Now . . .
(Looks at audience)
Who can I throw it at?
(Threatens several people)
Aha! Look who's coming! Don't say a word . . .
(Hides pie behind back)

(Enter girl)

            Hello!

Girl   Hello. I'm bored. I've got nothing to do.

Boy   Oh great! So am I. But I've got an idea for a game.

Girl   Really?

Boy   Yep. You close your eyes, count to ten, and I'll hide. Then you open your eyes and see if you can find me.

(Girl closes her eyes. Boy attempts to throw the pie.)

Girl	*(Opening her eyes)* Did you say count to ten?
Boy	*(Quickly hiding the pie again)* Yes!
Girl	One . . . two . . . *(She opens her eyes again)* What comes after two?
Boy	*(Hiding the pie yet again)* Three!
Girl	Oh yes. Three . . .

(Boy throws the pie in her face.)

	Ugh!
Boy	*(Laughs)* Hey, that was brill! I love throwing custard pies.
Girl	No it wasn't – it was horrible. *(She wipes her face)*
Boy	I know! I like being nasty and getting into trouble.
Girl	Well, you'd better be careful, because one day you might go too far.
Boy	No I won't.
Girl	Oh yes you will.
Boy	Oh no I won't . . . *(He gets the audience to join in)*
Boy	Alright, I'll tell you what. Close your eyes and I'll give you a present to say I'm sorry.

(Girl does so. Boy produces another pie and pushes it in her face.)

Girl	Oh! YOU . . .

(She slaps him and starts to throttle him. She stops when she sees he is standing with his arms stretched out.)

Boy	What's wrong?
Girl	I just remembered something. You remind me of Jesus standing like that . . . I'm sorry I hit you.

Boy   What about Jesus? Tell me, tell me – or I'll give you
             another pie!

Girl   Well, he died for all the things we do wrong . . .
             (She picks up a book from her bag)
             It's all in here, I heard it at Sunday School yesterday . . .

Boy   Well, tell me, tell me!

Girl   Alright – but only if you can do this.

(She begins to click with her fingers. He joins in, and encourages the audience to do the same. When the rhythm is going the girl begins. The boy gets the audience to echo each line.)

Girl   Jesus Christ is the Son of God.

(All echo this, led by the boy.)

             He was born as a baby for you and me.
             (She mimes holding baby)
             He walked around and did good things,

(She walks in time to the rhythm. The boy follows.)

             He even made a blind man see.

(Boy places his hands over his eyes, then removes them – eyes wide.)

Boy   Wow! Does it say that? Cor, Jesus is great!

Girl   When people were ill he made them well.

(Echo continues)

             He calmed the storms and walked on the sea.

(Walk in rhythm)

             He told them all about God's love.

(Point upwards)

             He cared for people like you and me.

(Point to audience)

(Act this next part out, with the boy being crucified, but still repeating the lines.)

             But they didn't like what Jesus said.
             (Girl accuses boy)
             They were afraid and they wanted him dead!
             (Grabs him)

They nailed him to a cross of wood.

(Boy mimes being nailed to a cross, flinching, and stops echoing words.)

He'd done no wrong, he'd just been good.
Jesus prayed God would forgive us,
For all the things that we do wrong.
And then he died and they took him down.

(Boy lies on the floor)

And they laid his body in the ground.
But three days later he came back to life,

(Boy jumps up and echoes the words again)

Early in the morning – 'bout a quarter to five!

(Look at watch)

And Jesus is alive today.
Let's follow him, now – what do you say?

Boy   Did they really do that to Jesus? Kill him like that? That's horrible! I guess the people went too far when they did that to Jesus.

Girl   Yes, but it was alright in the end – because God brought Jesus back to life and now we can be forgiven for the wrong things we do.

Boy   Like throwing custard pies? I'm sorry . . .

Girl   Oh, I don't mind too much about that. But remember, Jesus does want us to care for others, as well as having fun.

Boy   Yea . . . Hey, come on, we'd better go – my mum's tidied the house and we can have great fun getting it messy again!

Girl   Did you hear what I said?

Boy   Oh alright, just a little bit messy then, come on . . .

(They exit)

Harvest Gifts

A simple sketch about the way we can give our lives to God. It's especially appropriate for a Harvest or Christmas family service.

Cast   Dave
Simon

The two children should be played by adults. They are scruffy, chewing gum, pulling their clothes, scratching etc. While they talk they mess about with their school ties (if they have them), and saunter around the stage. The dialogue is written for two boys, but with a few changes it would suit two girls.

The two enter together.

Dave	'Ere, my mum said that we've got to go to church on Sunday.
Simon	*(With a big smile)* I know.
Dave	My mum said that we've got to go because it's Harvest *(or Christmas, Easter or another festival)* Sunday.
Simon	I know!
Dave	My mum said that we've got to take something to give to God to say 'Thank you'.
Simon	I know.
Dave	Well . . . what you gonna take then?
Simon	*(Pause. With a cheeky grin)* Guess.
Dave	I dunno . . . a sprout!
Simon	Nope.
Dave	A bag of carrots.
Simon	Nope.
Dave	*(Hopefully)* Not that conker you beat me with last week?
Simon	Don't be stupid! Course not.
Dave	I know – your Batman T-shirt!

Simon	*(Looks inside his jumper)* Nope.
Dave	Not your BMX bike?
Simon	Something much better than all of that.
Dave	But there isn't anything better than that.
Simon	Oh yes there is.
Dave	Oh no there isn't! *(Repeat this, involving the audience)*
Dave	What then?
Simon	*(Another pause)* Me!
Dave	But you can't give yourself to God on Harvest Sunday!
Simon	Oh yes I can.
Dave	Oh no you can't. *(Repeat again)*
Dave	Alright then – how?
Simon	Easy. Easy-peasy-lemon-squeezy! I'll tell you. *(Takes a deep breath)* I'm gonna ask God if I can be His best friend – and I'm gonna let Him be mine!
Dave	You mean – your bestest, bestest friend?
Simon	Yep – my bestest-bestest-everest friend!
Dave	Wow!

(Both freeze)

Friends

by Rory Browne

A sketch focusing on the need for friendship, and the way that Jesus can be our closest friend.

Cast   Narrator
A group of four to eight children or adults who respond to the narration with the actions in brackets

Begin with the Narrator alone on stage.

Narrator   It's good to have friends.

(All run in, laughing and talking)

It can be fun,

(Play leap frog and other playground games)

It can also be . . . well, rather boring.

(Yawn, look bored)

We can laugh together,

(All laugh with a partner)

We can cry together.

(Cry on each others' shoulders)

We often have a best friend

(Two of the group act like dogs. The others pair off.)

I didn't say 'Man's best friend'!

(The 'dogs' look sheepish as if being told off)

But friendship doesn't just happen – it takes time,

(Look at watches, rotate heads)

We have to work at it.

(Mime digging with shovels)

We often have to carry our friends through the storms;

(Make wind and storm sounds, one carries friend through)

We have to give a great deal

(Empty pockets)

Of ourselves.

(Kneel and offer open arms)

    Friendship has its ups and downs

(Bob up and down)

    And its downs and ups.

(Continue to bob, but out of time)

    A perfect friend . . .

(Look smug)

    Is impossible to find!

(Look crestfallen)

    Because we all have faults

(Look each other over, pick fleas)

    And no one is perfect – except . . .

(All look up sharply)

    For one person.

(Hands over eyes, scan audience)

    He offers a perfect friendship.

(All look up silently)

    He can be fun,

(All joke around)

    He laughs with us,

(All laugh)

    He cries with us;

(All cry)

    He spent his whole life working at making friends with us.

(Work hard, mop brow)

    He understands our ups and downs –

(Bob up and down randomly)

    He is in fact the perfect friend . . .

(Look surprised)

But before I introduce him, there is just one more thing
. . . This man not only gave of himself,

(Offer open arms to audience)

He lived his life for us,

(Raise arms slowly, embracing)

And finally . . .

(All now stand in crucifixion pose)

He died for us.

(All drop heads)

Let me introduce you to

(Narrator steps forward)

Jesus Christ –

(Narrator holds out his hand towards the group)

The only Son of God, our best friend.

(All freeze)

Out of the Mouths of Children

A sketch based on the healing of Jairus' daughter.

Cast   Teacher
Four or more children (who may be played by children or
adults) of whom two are called Julian and Cynthia

*The scene is the monthly family service in church. The teacher may be
male or female -- whoever it is they have difficulty maintaining control.*

*The children stand in a straggly line looking awkward. This piece is
fairly lively, but when it reaches the point when Cynthia faints this
should be done as realistically as possible, with Cynthia looking
increasingly ill as the sketch progresses.*

Teacher   Now children, today in the family service we're going to
tell the grown-ups a story.
(Smiles benignly at the congregation)

Children   Don't want to!

Teacher   *(Laughing it off)*
Yes you do. Of course you do. You can all help me to tell
it. It was the one we had last week in Sunday School,
remember?

Julian   Yea, I do – the one about Rambo and the chainsaw!

*(The children all join in with this idea, and demonstrate it
enthusiastically.)*

Teacher   *(To audience)*
Sorry about this - they're lovely children really.

(They all stop abruptly)

Children   No we're not!
(All pull faces at the audience)

Teacher   Ahem . . . yes, well, on with the story. Now, once upon a
time there was a little girl called Naomi . . .

*(The children all stick their thumbs in their mouth with comments like
'Goo goo!'.)*

Teacher   *(Getting slightly irritated)*
Not that little! She was about twelve . . .

(They start to fight and pull each other's hair)

Teacher *(Hastily)*
She was very well behaved!

Children Oh no she wasn't!

Teacher Oh yes she was!

Children Oh no she wasn't . . .
(They try to encourage the audience to join in)

Teacher That's enough!

Children *(Still in sing-song)*
Oh no it's not!

Teacher *(Shouts)*
QUIET!

(Cynthia blows a loud raspberry)

Teacher Who did that?

(All immediately step away from the culprit, point and shout:)

Children Cynthia did!

Teacher Did you Cynthia?

Cynthia *(Cheekily)*
Can't remember!

Teacher Right – in the corner! NOW!

(Cynthia reluctantly goes. The others giggle. The teacher ignores the children and ploughs on, addressing the audience.)

Teacher Now her father was called . . .

Children *(Cutting in)*
Dougal!

Teacher Jairus! He was called Jairus.

Julian I bet he was called Dougal really . . .

Cynthia *(Looking worried)*
Sir!

Teacher Be quiet – all of you. Now Jairus was very important . . .

Cynthia So is this, sir!

Teacher He was a Roman official . . .

Cynthia Sir, I don't feel very well!

Teacher   You should have thought of that before misbehaving. It's your own fault – don't blame me. Now, I don't want any more interruptions. We're trying to tell the adults an important story. Where was I . . .

(Cynthia looks as if she is about to faint)

Children   Please, sir . . .

Teacher   Now one day . . .

(Cynthia faints and collapses. The others rush round her. The teacher doesn't notice and continues valiantly.)

Teacher   She fell ill! Very ill! There was no hope for her – her father was so desperate that he even sent for Jesus to come and help . . .

(During this story Cynthia remains unconscious, despite attempts to help her. One of the children calls the others to pray. They kneel with their hands together. This all takes place silently. The teacher has not noticed.)

Teacher   But it was all too late – and by the time Jesus arrived, Naomi was dead. But Jesus didn't seem to bother about that, he took her by the hand and told her to get up!

(The children do this with Cynthia, she opens her eyes and wakes)

Teacher   Do you know – Jesus healed her completely! And he can do the same things today. Don't you believe that children? *(He turns to them for the first time. Cynthia is back on her feet, looking much better.)*

Children   *(With conviction)*
OH YES, SIR, WE DO!

Teacher   Good. Good.
(Smiles at adults, then turns to the children, and speaks sternly)
Now what was all the noise about? What's the problem?

(The children look at each other and shrug)

Julian   *(Innocently)*
Problem, what problem, sir? Tell us that story again – we liked it!

(All freeze)

The Party

A lively version of the parable of the wedding banquet.

Cast   King
         Queen
         Two or more servants

Both characters – the King and Queen – should be slightly over the top. Some sort of costume may be used; and as many props and servants as necessary. The servants are there to add energy and colour to the piece but be careful this does not distract from the dialogue.

The guests invited are all currently topical, but these names should be updated whenever necessary.

King	Oh dear – I feel very bored today. What can we do?
Queen	I know – I'll sing you a song! *(She begins)*
King	Oh no, no, please – that's awful. I mean, you mustn't strain your voice.
Queen	I know – how about a joke? What did the little chimney say to the big one.
King	I've heard it before.
Queen	Wrong! He said: you're too young to smoke! *(Laughs)* Get it? Or what do you call a gorilla with a machine gun?
King	Darling . . .
Queen	Wrong again – 'Sir!'
King	*(Leaping out of his seat)* I know! We'll have a party!
Queen	What?
King	Yes.

(He claps his hands twice, the servants run in)

Jelly and chips. Sausages and banana milk shakes. Fish fingers and ice cream. Ooh, I can taste it now. Who shall we invite?

(He claps his hands again and the servants become very active, rushing around and getting things ready. The more props they use the better. Other servants may enter the proceedings at this point.)

Queen	I know – the entire cast of 'Home and Away'.
King	Do be serious! We'll have just two – Cody and Gaby.
Queen	But they're in 'Neighbours' – you're getting rather muddled.
King	Don't worry about that . . . Paul Daniels, he can do a few magic tricks.
Queen	Jeremy Beadle – he gets about a bit. He can bring some videos to watch.
King	Yes . . . and we'll play some games. Ooh – Lynford Christie, he'll be good at musical chairs. And Steven Hendry and that nice Anthea Turner. That's enough.
Queen	I'll go and phone them all. *(She exits)*
King	Pass the parcel, funny hats, whistles, prizes – grrrreat! *(He runs around moving things and getting it all ready)*
King	This is going to be a terrific . . .
Queen	*(Rushes back in)* She won't come!
King	Who? Cody or Anthea.
Queen	Both. Neither. Too busy!
King	Oh well . . . never mind, at least Gaby's coming . . .
Queen	*(Shakes head)* Sorry. She's having acting lessons.
King	Oh dear. I know – invite the rest of the cast.
Queen	I already tried – they're all having acting lessons.
King	Okay then, try . . . Des Lynham, he always gets invited to the best parties.
Queen	How does he do that? *(She leaves again)*

King Now chocolate and marmite sandwiches, must remember some of those and also the peanut butter trifle.

Queen *(Shouts from off stage)*
Lynford's practising his sprint start, and Steven's counting his money!

King Oh well, all the more food for us! Now where's my Take That record . . .
(The Queen runs back in)

Queen Des Lynham's buying a lottery ticket, Jeremy Beadle's been framed – and Paul Daniels has disappeared.

(The servants stop and watch quietly)

King *(Trying to take it all in)*
Who does that leave?

Queen *(Counts on her fingers)*
. . . you! Oh, and me too!

King What! But . . . but . . . but . . . but . . . This is terrible!
(He sits down sadly)

Queen Don't worry, I've got an idea. If all the important, famous people won't come – you should invite all the ordinary people – I bet they'd love to come to a party with you.

King *(Cheering up)*
Do you think so? You mean . . . if all those other people won't come – we could invite all these people here! Great!

(They both freeze)

Arfur and the Big Blunder

A monologue about the creation and the fall of mankind from Genesis chapters 1, 2 and 3.

Cast   Arfur, an angel

Arfur is a rather rough and ready character – not a typical angel, but a character with plenty of fun and enthusiasm. He should be suitably dressed: jeans, cap, waistcoat, braces.

As he relates his adventure, he does so with lots of action and drama.

(Enter Arfur the Angel, holding an apple)

Oh dear. Oh dear, oh dear, we've got real problems now, oh dear . . .

(He rushes one way then back the other)

Oh dear, oh dear . . . I hope I don't get the blame for this one.

(He tries to hide the apple under a chair. Then he sees the audience, looks at the apple, and shoves it up his shirt. He forces a laugh.)

Ha! Ha, ha, h-hello everyone, sorry to interrupt your little 'do' here - just a little crisis you know, just a tiny problem involving the sins of the world, oops! Drat! I wasn't supposed to tell anyone that!

(He hastily checks the doors to see if anyone is listening)

Now, look, don't tell anyone what I said, please! Only I don't want to get blamed for this one. I just happened to . . . catch this . . .

(He pulls out the apple, it has a bite taken out of it)

Another case of being in the wrong place at the wrong time – honest! I'm really good at that. Oh I'd better explain. Now, my name's Arfur, Arfur the Angel – no it's alright, you don't have to grovel. I was just having a sunbathe see – in the garden . . . you know about the garden don't ya? Oh, didn't I mention it? Oh beautiful it is, beautiful. Eden.

(Points offstage one way then changes his mind and points the other)

Much better than Centre Parks! I was there when it happened. From nothing – whoosh!

(He throws his arms out)

God had this idea – and before you could say 'Let's think it over and have a committee meeting about it while we watch Neighbours' – he'd gone and done it! There was the world – created from nothing. Not a box of lego in sight! The Lord was really in his element, I can tell ya –

poetry in motion. Creating flowers he was by the millions, butterflies, clouds, dew, the morning mist – all from a pinch of soil!

(He flicks his fingers)

We had to get a JCB to move the mountain of sapphires that suddenly appeared when he cleared his throat. Pretty clever, eh? Anyway – it took your breath away, it did, there was monkeys, lobsters, hamsters, spiders.

(He looks on his shoulder and splats one. He shivers.)

Ugh! I hate spiders!

(Wipes his hand on his trousers)

Why did he have to make spiders, why not strawberries with legs, or something nice – like flying Smarties? But no, no, it had to be spiders. Yuk! Oh, yea, and then there was the dinosaurs, only I don't think they're all they're cracked up to be, myself. I can't see any future in them!

Anyway, we get to day seven and you know what he invents – absolutely brilliant this – the 'lie in'. No, not the lion, that was day five, no, no – the 'lie in'; closely followed by the 'breakfast in bed'. Ah, sheer genius!

So there I was enjoying it all, wasn't I? That garden of Eden – absolutely beautiful it was – is! Well, was!

You see it happened like this, I was a bit worn out after watching the Boss create the world from a bit of spit and a bit of soil, well, you would be wouldn't you? So I thought I'd have a kip. There I was – with my head on the lion's back. Tame as anything they are – it's the hamsters you got to watch! Anyway, I was just having a quick yawn and a stretch when . . . suddenly this lands in my mouth.

(He holds up the apple)

Only I didn't take the bite out of it.

Honest! I don't even like Golden Delicious!

They knew they shouldn't have done it . . . The people, I'm talking about. God made them on day six. Adam and Eve – the pride of his creation. I mean – could you make a robot that plays football like *(Insert name of current football star)*, sings like *(Insert name of pop star)*, dances like Fred Astaire, eats like a horse, sleeps like a baby, and moves like a dream? No. But God did. Man and woman he called them. You know why? Well, after he'd made them he stepped back had a good look at them and said, 'Man! That's good!' Then he gave them everything he'd made on this whole beautiful world. All they had to do was not eat anything off this tree. Simple isn't it? Except that Eve's got this thing about vitamin C – health food she calls it. So she decided to invent the first 'pick your own' orchard, and that changed everything. They went and blew it – just over some apple crumble. Now Adam sings like *(Football player)*, dances like a horse, plays football like Fred Astaire, eats like a pig and moves like a bulldozer! And the whole earth is slowly dying – all because Adam and Eve wanted some health food.

You see the problem ain't with the apple – God's got loads of them – but he told them not to do it. And that's what's wrong. When God tells you not to do something if you go and do it – that's a sin. It's nothing to do with Outspan! If we decide to go our own way, and not listen to the Boss – that's not right.

The sad thing is – everything's spoilt now. We got stinging nettles at the bottom of our garden – slugs eating our lettuces like there was no tomorrow – homework every night and school in the morning. And the animals? Well, you won't catch me sleeping with my head on a lion these days!

And poor old Adam – he just feels guilty all the time . . . it's very sad . . .

(He goes to leave then stops)

Mind you . . . I've heard a rumour. Plan B it's called.

God's got this idea – about a cross, and a man sort of nailed on it – sounds horrible to me! But I've heard whispers that if God could bring it off – it could make up for all them stinging nettles and sins and apples and things . . . Not a bad idea, eh?

(Looks round, then draws close to the audience)

I just wonder one thing about it though – I just wonder who they're gonna put on that cross?

(Exit)

Arfur the Angel's Greatest Assignment

Arfur's back! This time it's a monologue based on the account of Noah and the ark in Genesis chapters 6, 7 and 8.

Cast   Arfur, an angel

Arfur is a rather rough and ready character – not a typical angel, but a character with plenty of fun and enthusiasm. He should be suitably dressed: jeans, cap, waistcoat, braces.

As he relates his adventure, he does so with lots of action and drama.

(Enter Arfur. He sees the audience and makes straight for them. He begins to speak:)

Ah! There you are. Now, my name's Arfur – Arfur the Angel.

(He checks his appearance)

Now – I know I may not look like an angel, and you may not have heard of me, and I haven't got any wings . . . but I AM an angel. Take my word for it. And I've been sent here today by the Boss *(he looks up and raises his cap in respect)* to tell you about my greatest assignment. So listen hard – and listen good!

(He jumps on a nearby chair and begins his story – setting the scene with dramatic tones.)

There was a time . . . *(pause for effect)* when everyone was evil . . . and no one was good; and the world was very – dark!

(He squints and peers at the audience as if the room has suddenly been plunged into darkness.)

And people were very greedy!

(Grabs an imaginary chunk of food and chews it noisily)

And life was very – ugly!

(Pulls an ugly face and jumps off chair)

And nobody – but nobody – trusted in God.

(Pauses again for effect)

Now . . .

(Jumps back onto chair)

God – he was looking down on all this, and he was not happy . . . Until he noticed something.

(Looks down sharply and points, then exclaims:)

NOAH! He's different!

(Jumps off chair)

And that's where I come in. Next thing you know – I get a call from God.

(Walks to an imaginary or real phone and picks it up)

Hello? Arfur the Angel 'ere. Who is it? OH!

(Falls on his knees and hastily removes his cap)

Hello Lord. What? You got a job for me?

(Stands up again)

Oh right! Yea, Noah I know him. He's different? What – you mean he's had a haircut? He's changed his socks? No, I didn't think Noah would get round to doing that!

(Listens)

Oh! Oh you mean he's not like all the rest, he's not bad – in fact he's quite good? Right. Give me the lowdown, Lord – what do you want me to do?

(During the following instruction we see Arfur's response to some dramatic instructions from God. He becomes increasingly involved in the story which the Lord is relating.)

Right. Yea, you want me to . . . right, and then . . . okay, and then we'll have a lot of . . . whew! Okay, and then a few . . . and then – oh no! And then some more . . . with a bit of . . . and then I'll . . . right, right, and okay . . . and then – oh great! Yea, got it Lord. Oh, just one question – what's his phone number?

(Arfur replaces the phone and addresses the audience again)

So then – I – got on the blower – to Noah!

(Dials)

Earth – 01 – 390 – 55873632433987650654374312768541376654096878475482483747834383191085757939 – 1!
Hello? Is that Noah? Moses! Oh, sorry I've got the wrong number!

(To audience)

Eventually, I got through . . . Hello – is that Noah, it's Arfur the Angel here. What do you mean you've never heard of me? Well, no I haven't got any wings . . . but I AM an angel. I'm a distant relative of the Archangel Gabriel. Second cousin six times removed. Now listen. We've got a job for you. It's going to rain. Where are you going?

(Listens)

Don't worry about your washing, Noah, God wants you to build an ark. Oh, it's just a little boat, but don't worry about the details. You've got to take a few pets on board.

(He pulls a wad of paper from his pocket and lets it drop -- it is a very long list)

Rather a lot of pets in fact. 25,372 . . . Noah, are you alright . . . what do you mean joking, oh, oh chokin . . . I see! Oh well, breathe deeply a few times and put your head between your knees. Yes, you did hear correctly – we want two of every kind of animal. I'm afraid that does include spiders – yes! You see Noah – it's like this: man is bad, and God is good, and the two don't mix. So God's going to flood the earth. That's right Noah, with water. I wouldn't expect him to use diet coke, would you? And then, because God cares about the people, he's going to give them a choice. Either they can stop doing what they're doing, come inside the ark, and God can save them.

Or, they can carry on doing what they're doing, not come in the ark, *(Drops his voice sadly)* and God can't save them. In which case – they're going to get rather wet! Right, off you go then Noah, down to MFI! Oh, and don't forget the spiders!

(As he places the phone down) I hate spiders!

(He turns his head and sees one on his shoulder. He jumps and splats it with his hand.)

Ugh! Well, it's a long, long story, but God gave the people a choice: judgement . . . *(He holds his right hand out in a fist)* or mercy *(He holds his left hand out open)*.

Mercy meant that the people came in the ark and were saved. Judgement meant that the people refused to listen, and they . . .

(Splats another spider on his shoulder then looks at the remains on his hand)

died.

(He jumps back on the chair for the following announcement)

Ladies and gentlemen, only eight

(He holds up six fingers, then realises and adds two more)

people went into the ark. Only eight people were saved, along with all the animals of course. And when it was all over – Noah – was back on the blower.

(He picks up the phone again)

Hello, Arfur the Angel here.
Noah! Hello – well done! I've got a message for you from God.

(He pulls out a scrap of paper and clears his throat)

I am pleased to inform you that the Almighty is overflowing with extravagant mercy, exuberant joy, unconditional love, everlasting peace, eternal kindness and matchless grace towards his humble servant Noah.

(Noah hasn't managed to grasp all this)

I said: the Almighty is overflowing with extravagant mercy, unconditional love, exuberant joy, everlasting . . .

(He gives up and throws the note over his shoulder)

He's rather pleased with you, mate! How are all the animals then? Oh!

(To audience)

He's got rather a lot of rabbits! Well, never mind, you can open a pet shop. No, no I don't want to buy 135 tons of elephant dung, thanks. But I tell you what – if you've got that much – you can have a sale! Get it? A sail!

Never mind, Noah. Eh, did you get the message. Yea the rainbow. That's just a little reminder that God will never ever flood the earth again. Oh yes, it will rain again – but only at weekends and bank holidays! See ya.

(He puts down the phone)

What an assignment!

(Exit Arfur)

Note on Response Stories

Response stories are pieces which involve the whole audience (and the whole family); they are sketch-stories which can be used with little rehearsal or preparation. Each story contains four or more key words or phrases which are repeated at different points throughout the narrative. Whenever the audience/congregation hear the key words they should respond with the appropriate noise or action e.g. whenever the word 'Gideon' is said everyone should say: 'Who, me?'

The story may be presented by a narrator alone, or a whole group may lead the responses from the front – such a group may be rehearsed or spontaneous. The responses may also be written on cards and held up at the appropriate moments. However the piece is presented it should be done with vigour and enthusiasm, thus encouraging the audience to take part.

This book contains four of these pieces – 'Gideon', 'Nehemiah and the Builders', 'Wise Men' and 'Easter Morning' – but similar sketches can easily be created. Why not have a go yourself? Any Bible story, parable, or theme can be brought to life and understood using this simple, animated style of presentation. A balance needs to be struck with the key words in order that they are used frequently enough to keep the attention of the audience – but not so often that they become boring.

It may also be helpful if one or two of the words relate in some way to the point of the story, as it is these words that the audience is most likely to remember afterwards. Engaging parts of the audience in competition with each other is a good tool: e.g. who can make the most noise? The material for the stories may be lifted straight from the Bible as in 'Easter Morning'; or it may be modernised.

One other thought – do explain all the key words and responses clearly before you begin, as it can be frustrating for both the narrator and the audience if people long to join in but haven't quite grasped the whole picture. The responses in 'Nehemiah and the Builders' are more varied than in the other stories and so do need careful explanation.

Got the idea? Why not give it a try? These stories are excellent material for family services – and also good 'up your sleeve' routines for unexpected situations.

Gideon

The following sketch is designed to involve the whole audience, particularly the children. The story is narrated by one person, and at certain points the audience responds with appropriate noises or actions. The responses may be led by a group up front, and should be taught to the audience at the beginning.

Responses

Gideon	Who me?
Winepress	Squelch, squelch
Angel	Flap, flap (wings)
Frightened	Bite nails
Fleece	Baa!
Wet	Drip, drip, drip
Midianites	Boo
Smallest	Aah

There was once a young man called **GIDEON**.

Yes. And **GIDEON**, oh yes, worked in a **WINEPRESS**. And **GIDEON**, that's the one, didn't have a lot of courage, in fact, most of the time he was very **FRIGHTENED**, because he was the **SMALLEST** person in his family. But one day, while he was in the **WINEPRESS**, he saw an **ANGEL**, who said to him:

'Hello, **GIDEON**.'

'Yes, you,' said the **ANGEL**, 'I've got a job for you.'

'But I've already got one – in this **WINEPRESS**,' said **GIDEON**. And he was now very **FRIGHTENED**. After all, he was the **SMALLEST** person in his whole family.

The **ANGEL** replied, 'Now listen, **GIDEON**. Yes, you. I want you to go and fight the **MIDIANITES**.'

'The . . . the . . . the . . . **MIDIANITES**?' said **GIDEON**.

'Yes – YOU!'

'But the reason I'm in this **WINEPRESS,** is so that I can get away from the **MIDIANITES**. I mean, the **MIDIANITES,** are big . . . and bad! And I'm only the **SMALLEST** person in my family and, most important, I'm **FRIGHTENED**.'

'No need to be,' said the **ANGEL**, 'God will help you, **GIDEON**. Yes. You.'

But **GIDEON**, that's the one, was still very **FRIGHTENED**, so he had an idea. He decided to ask God to do something impossible, just to prove that God would help him.

'I've got this **FLEECE**,' he said to the **ANGEL**. 'If I put it on the ground, while I'm asleep can God make the **FLEECE WET**, but leave the ground dry? If he does that I'll know he can help me.'

So he laid out the **FLEECE** and went to bed.

And in the morning the **FLEECE** was **WET**, and Gideon, oh yes, was rather **FRIGHTENED**.

'Just to make sure, can I try it the other way round, so that God makes the ground **WET**, and the **FLEECE** dry? Then I'll really know that God's on my side.'

So he put the **FLEECE** down again and in the morning God had done it! So, **GIDEON** left the **WINEPRESS**, and even though he was small and **FRIGHTENED**, with a few other men he defeated all of the **MIDIANITES**, because God helped him.

Nehemiah and the Builders

This is a cross between a story and a sketch, and is told by one person with much audience participation. It tells the story of Nehemiah and his mission to rebuild the walls of Jerusalem, as found in Nehemiah chapters 2-6.

The responses should be taught to everyone before telling the story. The story may be read straight from the book, but if the script is learnt then it may be acted by the narrator, which will really bring the story to life.

Alternatively it may be presented as a sketch by a group and a narrator. To do this more actions may need to be added.

Responses

Hammer   Bang! Bang! Bang!

Saw   Zz! Zz! Zz!

Cement   Slop! Slop! Slop!

Plastering Splat! Splat! Splat!

Tea break Slu-u-u-urp!

Divide the audience into four sections, naming them North, South, East and West. Practice each section cheering as you call their name.

There are other, less frequent responses but these may easily be taught in the course of the story.

Some things are really difficult to do aren't they? Like . . . *(Think)* juggling! *(At this point produce three balls and attempt this. Whether you succeed or fail the audience will enjoy it if you do this with enthusiasm.)* Or . . . playing a musical instrument. *(Blow a whistle.)* Or adding 23,532.5 to 46,768.5. *(Scratch your head.)* But you know – God can help us with the difficult problems in life. Sometimes he even asks us to do difficult things – with his help. Like the story of Nehemiah! Now that's a difficult name! Neherm . . . Namun . . . Nanerm . . . Neh-em-i-ah! Fancy being called that!

Now, Nehemiah was a servant – in a place called Suza – he was a servant to the king there. But he hadn't always lived there – he used to live in Jerusalem, which was a beautiful city, surrounded by huge walls, that no one could see over. *(Attempt to see over an imaginary wall.)* And it had large gates. *(Use forearms as gates, and swing them shut in front of chest.)* Crash!

Now one day, while Nehemiah was doing his job, *(Take up the stance of a servant, tray in one hand, take a bow)* he met an old friend of his, so he asked him 'How are things in Jerusalem?' And do you know what? His friend told him that things were bad, because the city was in a mess. The walls had fallen down *(Look up at big walls, then look down as if they have collapsed)* and the gates were broken. *(Close gates in front of chest, then let forearms swing from the elbows.)*

And Nehemiah was very sad. So he did the one thing that he could do – he prayed! *(Adopt a praying stance.)* And God helped him! Before you could say 'Nehemiah-is-a-very-funny-name!', the king had told him that he could go back to Jerusalem to help them rebuild the walls. So – off he went. *(Jump and turn.)*

When he got there – the city was in a terrible mess! *(Look around in horror.)*

But God told Nehemiah to rebuild the city, so he set to work. He got all the people together, and sent them off to different parts of the wall.

Some went to the East *(Get the East to cheer)*,
Some to the West *(West cheer)*,
Some to the North *(North cheer)*,
And some to the South. *(South cheer)*

And then some began to **HAMMER** *(Hammering noise and action)*,
and some began to **SAW** *(Sawing noise and action)*,
and some mixed **CEMENT**,
and some did the **PLASTERING**.

Then the East **HAMMERED**, and the West **SAWED**, and the North mixed **CEMENT**, and the South did the **PLASTERING**. *(Get each part to do the relevant noise and action.)*

And then they all had a **TEA BREAK**. *(Mime blowing whistle and then slurp tea.)*

And then they went back to work. *(Repeat hammering, sawing, cementing and plastering noises and actions.)*

TEA BREAK!

Then they began to build the wall with bricks.

(Teach the following actions by numbers.)

1. TAKE BRICK *(Mime picking up a brick.)*

2. TAKE CEMENT *(Mime taking a trowel full of cement.)*

3. SPREAD IT *(Mime spreading it on a flat surface.)*

4. LAY BRICK *(Place the brick on the cement.)*

(Repeat these actions several times to the numbers.)

1-2-3-4   1-2-3-4   1-2-3-4   1-2-3-4

Now, there were some people who didn't like Nehemiah and they didn't want him to rebuild the walls. So when they saw all the **HAMMERING, SAWING, CEMENT** mixing, and **PLASTERING** they got very angry. And when the builders took a **TEA BREAK**, they tried to stop the work. They did all sorts of bad things.

They told lies about them.

'WHISPER, WHISPER'

(The group may repeat these responses.)

They made fun and laughed at them.

'Ner Ner – Ner Ner – Ner!'

(Pull faces)

They tried to make them stop.

(Shout)

'STOP!'

They even tried to knock it down.

(Mime pushing against the wall.)

But they couldn't – because Nehemiah prayed to God – and God helped them. Every day he prayed – and everyday God helped them. Until, after fifty two days – they had finished! And all the people gathered together – from the East, and West, and North, and South. Then they all cheered together (Cheer) and thanked God.

(You may like to end the story here, or add this last part.)

Then they listened as God's law was read out to them. When they heard it – they began to feel sad – and to cry, because they thought of all the wrong things they'd done in their lives, and they were very sorry.

But then Nehemiah said this: *(Jump on a chair)*

'Don't be unhappy! This is a marvellous day! God cares about us, and he's helped us to rebuild the wall. It's a time to celebrate and have a party because of all the good things God has done.'

And so the people cheered again *(Cheer)*. And Nehemiah told them this promise:

'The joy' *(Clap, clap)* 'of the Lord' *(Clap, clap)* 'is your strength.' *(Clap, clap)*

And that means that God will help us to be strong when we trust in him. And everyone said this:

'The joy' *(Clap, clap)* 'of the Lord' etc.

(Teach this to everyone and either say it together, or divide the group into North, South, East and West to say it.)

So remember, God can help us with the difficult things when we ask him – just like he helped Nehemiah.

(Exit)

Wise Men

A story with audience participation about the wise men in Matthew chapter 2.

The story is narrated by one person, and at certain points the audience responds with the appropriate noise or action as listed below.

Responses

Star	Twinkle, twinkle
Wise Men	Ding!
Herod	Boo
Camels	Appropriate camel noise e.g. Brrr!
Stable	(Half the audience) Moo (The other half) Baa
Journey	Clip, clop

Once upon a time there were three **WISE MEN**,
Who lived far away, way back when
CAMELS were the way to travel, not cars
And instead of maps they followed stars.

One day the **WISE MEN** had nothing to do
And their **CAMELS** were bored in their **STABLE** too,
When they all looked up and saw a **STAR**
Shining for a king in a country far.

Well, the **STAR** was moving so they decided to go
On a **JOURNEY** – but where they didn't know.
So they packed some peanut butter spread
And headed for the desert with the **STAR** up ahead.

On their **CAMELS** they rode along,
Followed the **STAR** till their sandwiches had gone.
And when their **JOURNEY** came to an end
They found themselves in Bethlehem.

Now being **WISE MEN** they went to **HEROD** the king,
He was the boss round there, and they told him

About the **JOURNEY**, and the **CAMELS** and the sandwiches too,
HEROD wasn't impressed – he was not a nice dude.

He told the **WISE MEN** to spill the beans,
And tell him if there really was a king to be seen.
But **HEROD** was bad – he wanted to kill the king,
The **WISE MENS' CAMELS** had more brains than him.

So they **JOURNEY**'d on and the **STAR** came to rest,
Over a **STABLE**, they were not impressed.
'Coz the **STABLE** was dirty – it smelt of **CAMELS** and hay,
But being **WISE MEN** they went in anyway.

And there amongst the animals they saw the king,
Just a tiny baby – but they worshipped him.
They all knelt down and gave him some gifts,
Then they left and decided to give **HEROD** a miss.

And there's a message for us to remember today,
At Christmas time there's a choice to be made.
We can be like **HEROD** – he never found the king,
Or like the **WISE MEN** – we can worship him.

Easter Morning

A story with audience participation about the resurrection account, John chapter 20.

The story is narrated by one person, and at certain points the audience responds with the appropriate noise or action as listed below.

Responses

Angel	Ding! (Point to halo)
Sad	Ahh!
Garden	Tree mime and bird noises
Spices	Rub fingers and sniff them
Alive	(Cheer) Hurray!
Name	(Shout) Mary

It all began very early on Sunday morning. Mary was on her way to the tomb with a jar of **SPICES**. She was feeling very **SAD**, because Jesus was a good friend of hers, and he was now dead.

She walked into the **GARDEN** with her jar of **SPICES**, and slowly and sadly made her way to the tomb. The **GARDEN** looked very beautiful early in the morning, but Mary felt so **SAD** that she hardly noticed. She really couldn't believe that Jesus was dead.

Suddenly, as she got near the tomb she heard a voice, calling her **NAME**. It was an **ANGEL**! A shining bright, dazzling **ANGEL**!

Well, Mary was so surprised that she dropped her **SPICES**, and she felt like running out of the **GARDEN** again.

The **ANGEL** spoke to her. 'Why are you so **SAD**? Jesus isn't here he's **ALIVE**!'

Mary was amazed when she heard this, and leaving the **ANGEL**, she ran out of the **GARDEN**, almost tripping over the jar of **SPICES**. She ran to the other disciples, and told them about the **ANGEL**. They were feeling very **SAD** too, and didn't believe her. So she took them right back to the **GARDEN**. Peter and John ran straight in, tripped over the **SPICES** – and saw the **ANGEL**! What a surprise.

'Why are you looking in a grave for someone who's **ALIVE**?' The **ANGEL** asked them.

Peter and John didn't know what to say to that, so they went into the tomb.

Meanwhile, outside in the **GARDEN**, Mary was still feeling confused and **SAD**. Could Jesus really be **ALIVE**? She looked for the **ANGEL**, but he had gone, so she bent down to pick up the **SPICES**. And that was when she saw the gardener.

'Have you taken him away?' Mary asked him.

The gardener didn't reply – but instead he called out her **NAME**.

As soon as Mary heard it she knew – he wasn't the gardener, this was Jesus. **ALIVE**! The moment she heard him say her **NAME** – she knew his voice. No longer **SAD**, she jumped up, left the **SPICES** and went running out of the **GARDEN**, to tell the others that Jesus was **ALIVE**!

When Peter and John came out of the tomb both Jesus and the **ANGEL** had gone. But Mary had seen them both – and she knew that Jesus really was **ALIVE**.

DAVE HOPWOOD
Drama and Mime Training

Trained in mime and physical theatre at the Desmond Jones School in London, and with many years' experience as an actor and mime artist, Dave now regularly runs training weekends, day conferences, evening classes and workshops all over the country in:

- mime technique
- writing drama material
- schools work
- street theatre
- directing
- choreography
- improvisation

He also produces a regular newsletter, **Adrenalin**, packed with resources and ideas.

Contact Dave at:

Christ Church, Church Street East, Woking Surrey GU21 1YG

Other drama books from
National Society/Church House Publishing

THE NATIONAL SOCIETY
A Christian Voice in Education

The National Society (Church of England) for Promoting Religious Education is a charity which supports all those involved in Christian education – teachers and school governors, students and parents, clergy and lay people – with the resources of its RE Centres, archives, courses and conferences.

Founded in 1811, the Society was chiefly responsible for setting up the nationwide network of Church schools in England and Wales and still provides grants for building projects and legal and administrative advice for headteachers and governors. It now publishes a wide range of books, pamphlets and audio-visual items, and two magazines, *Crosscurrent* and *Together*.

For details of membership of the Society or to receive a copy of our current catalogue please contact:

> The Promotions Secretary,
> The National Society,
> Church House,
> Great Smith Street,
> London
> SW1P 3NZ
> *Tel: 0171-222 1672*